AIMR Conference Proceedings
Equity Portfolio Construction

Proceedings of the AIMR seminar "The Future of Equity Portfolio Construction"

26–27 March 2002
Chicago

Theodore R. Aronson, CFA
Harold S. Bradley
Howard M. Crane, CFA
Richard M. Ennis, CFA
John D. Freeman, *moderator*

Ronald N. Kahn
Mark P. Kritzman, CFA
Burton G. Malkiel
Thomas K. Philips
Bruno Solnik

Association for Investment Management and Research®

Dedicated to the Highest Standards of Ethics, Education, and
Professional Practice in Investment Management and Research.

To obtain an *AIMR Product Catalog,* contact
AIMR, 560 Ray C. Hunt Drive, Charlottesville, Virginia 22903, U.S.A.
Phone 434-951-5499; Fax 434-951-5262; E-mail info@aimr.org
or
visit AIMR's Web site at www.aimr.org
to view the AIMR publications list.

CFA®, Chartered Financial Analyst™, AIMR-PPS®, GIPS®, and Financial Analysts Journal® are just a few of the trademarks owned by the Association for Investment Management and Research®. To view a list of the Association for Investment Management and Research's trademarks and the Guide for Use of AIMR's Marks, please visit our Web site at www.aimr.org.

©2002, Association for Investment Management and Research

All rights reserved. No part of this publication may be reproduced, stored in a retrieval system, or transmitted, in any form or by any means, electronic, mechanical, photocopying, recording, or otherwise, without prior written permission of the copyright holder.

AIMR CONFERENCE PROCEEDINGS
(USPS 013-739 ISSN 1535-0207) 2002, no. 5

Is published five times a year in March, April, twice in August, and September, by the Association for Investment Management and Research at 560 Ray C. Hunt Drive, Charlottesville, VA. **Periodical postage paid at Charlottesville, Virginia, and additional mailing offices.**

This publication is designed to provide accurate and authoritative information with regard to the subject matter covered. It is sold with the understanding that the publisher is not engaged in rendering legal, accounting, or other professional services. If legal advice or other expert assistance is required, the services of a competent professional should be sought.

Copies are mailed as a benefit of membership to CFA® charterholders. Subscriptions also are available at $100.00 USA. For one year. Address all circulation communications to AIMR Conference Proceedings, 560 Ray C. Hunt Drive, Charlottesville, Virginia 22903, USA; Phone 434-951-5499; Fax 434-951-5262. For change of address. Send mailing label and new address six weeks in advance.

Postmaster: Please send address changes to AIMR Conference Proceedings, Association for Investment Management and Research, P.O. Box 3668, Charlottesville, Virginia 22903.

ISBN 0-935015-87-6
Printed in the United States of America
September 12, 2002

Editorial Staff
Kathryn Dixon Jost, CFA
Editor

Maryann Dupes	Jaynee M. Dudley
Book Editor	*Production Manager*
Sophia E. Battaglia	Donna C. Hancock
Assistant Editor	*Production Coordinator*
Rebecca L. Bowman	Kelly T. Bruton
Assistant Editor	Lois A. Carrier
	Composition

Contents

Foreword iv
    Kathryn Dixon Jost, CFA

Biographies v

Overview 1
    John D. Freeman

Views of an "Informed" Trader 5
    Harold S. Bradley

How Much Diversification Is Enough? 18
    Burton G. Malkiel

Global Considerations for Portfolio Construction 29
    Bruno Solnik

Growth and Value Investing: Understanding the Sources of Excess Returns 38
    Thomas K. Philips

Reintegrating the Equity Portfolio 50
    Richard M. Ennis, CFA

What Plan Sponsors Need from Their Active Equity Managers 57
    Ronald N. Kahn

The Role of Benchmarks in the 21st Century 66
    Howard M. Crane, CFA

Innovations in Risk Measurement 76
    Mark P. Kritzman, CFA

Selected Publications 90

Foreword

Lumber, nails, concrete, electrical wires, pipes—just a few of the materials needed to construct a building. But constructing a building requires more than the raw materials. An architect first draws the building plans; a structural engineer reviews the plans; and a contractor hires the foreman and the construction workers with the expertise to implement the plans. Only after these steps have been completed do the raw materials enter the process.

Constructing an equity portfolio similarly requires more than the raw materials, more than the stock holdings. As with a building, constructing a portfolio requires design work, technical analysis, and skilled personnel to implement the plan, and again, only after these steps have been taken do the raw materials (stocks) enter the picture. The authors in this proceedings can be thought of as designers, technical analysts, and skilled managers overseeing the construction process. Their presentations focus on achieving best execution for a portfolio, structuring for sufficient diversification, finding added value, properly choosing benchmarks, and controlling portfolio risk. Each author emphasizes that, although the basic building blocks of an equity portfolio (the stocks) are important, the process for constructing the portfolio is even more important.

We greatly appreciate all the hard work the authors put into their presentations, so in recognition of that hard work, we would like to thank Harold S. Bradley, American Century Ventures; Burton G. Malkiel, Princeton University; Bruno Solnik, HEC School of Management; Thomas K. Philips, Paradigm Asset Management Company; Richard M. Ennis, CFA, Ennis Knupp + Associates; Ronald N. Kahn, Barclays Global Investors; Howard M. Crane, CFA, Watson Wyatt Investment Consulting; and Mark P. Kritzman, CFA, Windham Capital Management Boston. We would also like to give special thanks to John D. Freeman of Freeman Associates Investment Management LCC for serving as moderator at the conference and writing the overview for this proceedings.

Whether making sand castles or houses of cards, the fascination for building and constructing starts at a young age. And the authors in this proceedings have not lost that zeal for construction—albeit equity portfolio construction.

Kathryn Dixon Jost, CFA
Vice President
Educational Products

Biographies

Harold S. Bradley is president of American Century Ventures, a wholly owned subsidiary corporation of American Century Companies, and is a member of the investment oversight committee for American Century Investments. He also directed the American Century equity trading group and served as a mutual fund portfolio manager. Previously, Mr. Bradley was a member of the Kansas City Board of Trade and served as marketing director of its exchange. He also serves on the Investment Company Institute Task Force on Market Structure and frequently contributes to *Traders Magazine* about issues facing buy-side investors. Mr. Bradley is a graduate of Marquette University.

Howard M. Crane, CFA, is the North American practice director for Watson Wyatt Investment Consulting. Previously, he was a senior consultant and director of consulting practice at Frank Russell Company, headed BT Consulting at Bankers Trust Company, managed the Financial Advisory Service Division at Chase Manhattan Bank, and began the Analytical Services Division at the Northern Trust Company in Chicago. Mr. Crane serves as an adjunct professor and sits on the Business Advisory Board at the University of Washington at Tacoma. He completed his undergraduate work and his master's degree in operations research at Union College and holds a master's degree in economics from Brown University.

Richard M. Ennis, CFA, is principal and chairman of the board of directors of Ennis Knupp + Associates, where he consults with clients and directs the firm's investment policy research. Previously, he was affiliated with A.G. Becker, O'Brien (now Wilshire) Associates and Transamerica Investment Management Company. Mr. Ennis has served as an expert witness in fiduciary and investment litigation, and his research has been published in such journals as the *Financial Analysts Journal* and the *Journal of Portfolio Management*. His real estate research received the *Financial Analysts Journal* Graham and Dodd Award in 1991. Mr. Ennis holds a B.S. from California State University at Northridge and an M.B.A. from the University of California at Los Angeles.

John D. Freeman is president of Freeman Associates Investment Management LLC, where he oversees investment strategies, product research, and client relations. He also heads the firm's investment committee and serves as a portfolio manager. Previously, Mr. Freeman was a vice president and portfolio manager at Martingale Asset Management and a manager of consulting services at Barra. He serves on the advisory committee of the *Journal of Investing* and has published numerous articles, primarily dealing with implementation and execution of investment strategies.

Ronald N. Kahn is managing director and head of active equities at Barclays Global Investors (BGI). Before joining BGI, he was director of research at Barra, where his research spanned the equity and fixed-income markets in the United States and globally. Mr. Kahn co-authored, with Richard Grinold, *Active Portfolio Management: Quantitative Theory and Applications*. He is on the editorial advisory boards of the *Journal of Portfolio Management* and the *Journal of Investment Consulting*. Mr. Kahn holds an A.B. in physics from Princeton University and a Ph.D. in physics from Harvard University and was a postdoctoral fellow in physics at the University of California at Berkeley.

Mark P. Kritzman, CFA, is managing partner of Windham Capital Management Boston and a senior partner of State Street Associates. He is the research director of the AIMR Research Foundation and serves on the boards of the Institute for Quantitative Research in Finance and the International Securities Exchange, as well as on the editorial boards of the *Financial Analysts Journal, Journal of Alternative Investments*, and *Journal of Derivatives*. Mr. Kritzman has written numerous articles for academic and professional journals and is the author of six books, including *The Portable Financial Analyst* and *Puzzles of Finance*. He holds a B.S. from St. John's University and an M.B.A. with distinction from New York University.

Burton G. Malkiel is Chemical Bank Chairman's Professor of Economics at Princeton University and is the author of the widely read investment book *A Random Walk Down Wall Street*. Previously, he was dean of the Yale School of Organization and William S. Beinecke Professor of Management Studies at Yale. Professor Malkiel is a past appointee to the Council of Economic Advisors and past president of the American Finance Association. He is a director of such organizations as the Vanguard Group of Investment Companies and the Prudential Insurance Company of America. Professor Malkiel holds a B.A. and an M.B.A. from Harvard University and a Ph.D. from Princeton University.

Thomas K. Philips is chief investment officer at Paradigm Asset Management Company, where he is responsible for all aspects of the investment process, including the development of new products and the enhancement of existing ones. Previously, he was managing director at RogersCasey and worked at IBM Corporation in research and in active equity management for the IBM Thomas J. Watson Research Center and the IBM Retirement Fund. Mr. Philips is the author of several journal papers and book chapters on topics in finance, engineering, and mathematics. He holds an M.S. and a Ph.D. in electrical and computer engineering from the University of Massachusetts at Amherst.

Bruno Solnik is professor and chair of finance and economics at HEC School of Management. Previously, he served on the faculty of the Stanford Business School and has been a visiting professor at the University of California at Berkeley and at Los Angeles and the Université de Genève. Professor Solnik is the author of seven books, including *International Investments*, and numerous articles in such leading journals as the *Journal of Finance* and the *Financial Analysts Journal*. He also serves on the editorial boards of several major finance journals. Professor Solnik received the *Financial Analysts Journal* Graham and Dodd Award in 1994. He holds an engineering degree from Polytechnique in Paris and a Ph.D. from Massachusetts Institute of Technology.

Overview: Equity Portfolio Construction

John D. Freeman
Freeman Associates Investment Management LLC
Rancho Santa Fe, California

> Experience isn't what happens to you; experience is what you do with what happens to you.
>
> Aldous Huxley

Investment managers often succumb to the fallacy of composition, believing that their portfolio of attractive stocks must form an attractive portfolio. While so-called informal fallacies, such as fallacies of composition, do not necessarily violate rules of logic, the reasoning behind them may be hasty and inconclusive. Portfolio managers' obsession with security valuation tends to obscure critical issues of portfolio construction, issues that ultimately determine whether a portfolio is attractive or not.

If active managers and active portfolios were systematic and unbiased, investors would never again have to hear of good (bad) periods for active management just as they would never hear about good (bad) periods for gravity, daylight, or adherence to the Bill of Rights. The counterproductive boom/bust cycles of active management have been around for years, with the advent of index funds representing one seminal solution to this problem.

Undoubtedly, the ensuing emphasis on investment benchmarks and the proliferation of passive alternatives have increased the speed and severity of this boom/bust cycle. Despite the nearly 20 years required statistically to ascertain active management skill, portfolio managers are subject to termination well short of a single market cycle, perhaps after one or two rocky quarters. Manager terminations often appear to be undertaken lightly by plan sponsors and consultants, even though they are expensive and time consuming.

Investors have to look no farther back than the great "growth" market to find a time when insightful but less structured value managers were hemorrhaging client assets, much of which went into index funds and other low-risk strategies. Subsequently, the same managers experienced tremendous runs of active performance, but the assets managed in a less-active manner failed to participate symmetrically in the active recovery. This was a bittersweet result for active managers, consultants, and plan sponsors alike.

With all of the time, energy, and high stakes devoted to success in portfolio management, one might contend that discussions in this field would be tilling tired soil. Nothing could be further from the truth. The insights offered by the authors are neither old hat nor pie in the sky. They reflect the intelligence, the training, and above all, experience of top academicians, investment consultants, portfolio managers, and traders. Some of their insights may seem contradictory. In fact, at times they are. Each author brings a different perspective to the aggregate problem. A good point of departure is market efficiency. One author suggests that efficient equity markets are a good place to begin—and end. Another introduces opportunities for active returns—in small doses (combined with heaps of passive strategies) unconstrained by style boxes, tracking error, or any of the other analytical barbed wire that might fence off high-value-added possibilities.

Many portfolio managers continue to fight against benchmarks as encroachments on their investment authority. But benchmarks are not constraints any more than a map is a constraint. Benchmarks help portfolio managers, their clients, and consultants more accurately and expeditiously demarcate intent and omission, insight and oversight. Those who are talented, those who can add value without exposing the client to undue risk, receive substantial payoffs. And finally, risk is not just about where investors might find themselves at the end of the journey but, rather, about the depth and frequency of the potholes along the way.

Best Execution

Thanks to advances in technology, opportunities have arisen for investors to change the way orders are routed, secure lower trading costs, and enhance investment returns. In Harold Bradley's view, however, only those investors who are vigilant about best-execution practices and who are willing to invest time in figuring out how stocks are actually traded will be able to update their trading methods and adapt to the use of new electronic trading technologies to truly achieve best execution. Accordingly, he carefully outlines how orders are handled in the auction market currently in place and illustrates how investors, who daily face the arcane, anticompetitive rules of member-owned exchanges, stand to benefit from the greater efficiency and equality provided by electronic communications networks.

In addition, Bradley emphasizes that brokerage firms will have to do more than merely invest in new technologies; they will also have to devise better ways to track the adequacy of their order-handling systems and the timeliness of their execution reports. Because of a major shift in the way the U.S. SEC and industry standard setters (such as AIMR) are looking at best-execution practices, he recommends that firms establish trade management oversight committees to measure trade efficacy and be prepared to answer questions regarding trade transparency, record keeping, and accountability.

Diversification

In addition to facing changes regarding best execution, investors are finding that achieving adequate diversification is more difficult now than in the past. Burton Malkiel documents this challenge by pinpointing two areas in which portfolio selection theory and practice have diverged. First, because idiosyncratic risk has risen and will likely continue to rise, investors now require a larger number of stocks to eliminate idiosyncratic risk from their portfolios than they did in the 1960s. Second, because global markets have become much more highly correlated in the past 10 years, investors may not get as much diversification benefit from non-U.S. stocks as was previously thought (which is not to say, however, that active managers should not still invest in non-U.S. stocks and try to take advantage of valuation differences between U.S. and non-U.S. stocks or of currency realignments—i.e., the weakening U.S. dollar).

Given these developments, Malkiel recommends that investors add REITs (real estate investment trusts) and Treasury Inflation-Indexed Securities to the traditional portfolio of stocks, bonds, and T-bills. And because of the overwhelming evidence that index funds continue to outperform most actively managed funds, he advocates making index funds a basic element in portfolios. By incorporating nontraditional asset classes into portfolios, reevaluating the trend against lowered allocations to non-U.S. stocks, and making indexing (particularly total stock market index funds) a core component of their investing strategy, investors will be more likely to achieve sufficient diversification and thereby improve portfolio performance.

The question of international diversification is the focus of Bruno Solnik's thought-provoking presentation. Now that nearly all corporations seem to be thinking, and operating, globally and correlations between countries have increased, a reevaluation of the whole structure of international investing is in order. Country factors, for example, are still important, but if a company is conducting extensive international activities, it should be valued, in an efficient market, as an international portfolio of activities. Indeed, his research shows that the percentage of international activity of a company dictates its exposure to the various regional factors.

Solnik analyzes his most recent finding that industry factors (as opposed to country factors) are increasingly affecting company stock prices. He argues that managers should use neither the traditional "balance sheet" nor the "multinational" approach to international investing. Industry-specific and company-specific analysis must take precedence over country-specific analysis. Therefore, in Solnik's opinion, to ask what percentage of a portfolio should be invested internationally is a moot question. Instead, investors should recognize the pervasive implications of globalization and begin applying a "cross-industry, cross-country" approach that takes advantage of global sector influences and provides opportunities for superior return and risk management.

Finding Added Value

While keeping pace with advances in technology and the myriad changes in the global markets, investors must continuously reevaluate the strategies and techniques behind equity portfolio construction in order to find value-added opportunities. To that end, Thomas Philips' analysis of index construction sheds light on the issue of growth versus value investing. Although the definition of value investing has not changed much since Benjamin Graham first started touting the practice, the academic approach to defining value no longer corresponds to the way managers actually invest. Indeed, the line between growth and value investing is far from distinct in practice, and determining the source of value in value investing is no easy task.

According to Philips' "Fundamental Theorem of Growth Equality," the equality of growth rates of value and growth stocks is very strong, largely because of the index construction methodology of growth and value indexes. As a result, if both types of indexes have the same long-run rate of earnings growth (and if a P/E bubble does not occur), the capital gains component of return for the indexes must be identical and any difference in return between them is simply a result of the difference in their dividends or dividend equivalents. Through concrete examples, Philips illustrates the implications of his findings: Free cash flow yields (i.e., dividends and dividend equivalents) matter much more than most investors think they do, and the expected value premium is about one-quarter of a percent.

Another provocative issue worth exploring is whether a new "architecture" is warranted for managing portfolios. Richard Ennis argues that big pension funds and other diversified institutional investors should adopt a whole-stock rather than a multiple-specialist portfolio approach. He maintains that reintegrating equity portfolio management through the use of whole-stock portfolios is better for clients because it reduces costs, provides more value-added opportunities, and removes the burden on clients to become active participants in portfolio construction.

Although the multiple-specialist model provides several advantages, Ennis demonstrates how equity product differentiation and proliferation have served the interests of managers at the expense of clients. In his view, the conventional model has minimal benefits compared with the advantages of adopting a whole-stock approach, which is characterized by breadth, freedom, and completeness. For example, by being able to exploit value-adding opportunities in all market-cap and style bands, managers can avoid the "style boxes" that constrain their investing opportunities. Furthermore, not only are the techniques for defining style categories imperfect, but the less-than-perfect characterizations of manager styles have also created performance measurement problems for managers and have contributed significantly to so-called misfit risk. Globalization poses additional challenges for the multiple-specialist model, and Ennis raises the question of whether maintaining a domestic versus foreign distinction in an efficiently managed portfolio still makes sense.

For active equity managers wondering about the value of risk budgeting, Ronald Kahn provides a quantitative analysis of what plan sponsors need from managers and what managers should be able to provide in terms of processes and risk controls. In short, drawing on Richard Grinold's Fundamental Law of Active Management, he shows that plan sponsors need consistent outperformance (i.e., high information ratios) from their managers. Plan sponsors can maximize the expected alpha given their risk budget by allocating their risk budget in proportion to information ratios. Managers, in turn, can construct investment products that will produce the requisite high information ratios. From the plan sponsor's perspective, those products that combine wide breadth, a high level of skill, and efficient strategies (i.e., those not unduly affected by the long-only constraint) are the most appealing; generally, risk-controlled long-only and aggressive long–short products work better than the more inefficient high-risk, long-only strategies.

Kahn follows his analysis of what plan sponsors need with several examples that illustrate how risk budgeting works. He recommends a bottom-up approach: By beginning with an analysis of a plan's current product and risk allocations rather than a determination of what the risk budget should be, the plan sponsor can calculate the plan's current risk level. Then, assuming that this amount of risk is acceptable and that the plan sponsor is happy with its current managers, the optimal allocations to each of these managers can be appropriately determined. Kahn warns, however, that because the ideas that have created outperformance in the past may not work well in the future, determining where alpha will come from is possible only through continuing investment in research on this topic.

Benchmarks and Risk Measurement

New approaches to portfolio construction and new definitions of risk have evolved to help solve the overarching problem of portfolio construction and risk measurement, a task that Howard Crane regards as the main challenge of the future. In his presentation, he thus focuses on illustrating why the effective use of benchmarks—which are vital to the asset planning cycle, portfolio structure and risk control processes, and integrated solutions for risk budgeting—is the key to investment success. Specifically, Crane addresses the dilemma that as benchmarks continue to evolve, investment managers will struggle to find opportunities for outperformance.

Because the fund management process promises to remain dynamic, Crane's review of the eight stages of the asset planning cycle can help clients understand the risks inherent in benchmarks and the trade-offs in choosing a benchmark. As the industry moves away from managing to the benchmark and from using tracking error as a measure of risk, he recommends that managers create proprietary benchmarks to improve investment efficiency in portfolio construction and portfolio measurement. Finally, Crane's integrated solution to risk budgeting clearly outlines five progressive steps to align the asset allocation process with the risk allocation process. Although he emphasizes that there is no such thing as a perfect benchmark, he concludes that various structural alternatives for benchmark and portfolio construction exist that require qualitative, not just quantitative, appraisal.

Significant developments in risk management also portend substantial changes in the way managers, analysts, and investors should assess risk in constructing portfolios. Mark Kritzman makes the case that portfolio risk is largely underestimated because of two particular shortcomings in the assumptions underlying portfolio construction: the focus on end-of-period risk to the exclusion of within-horizon risk and the tendency to regard asset allocation as more important than security selection.

To overcome the inadequacy of current risk measures, Kritzman proposes a method that captures an investor's exposure to loss not only at the end of the investment horizon but also throughout the investment period. His formula for determining the probability of loss throughout an investment period, including at the end, called "continuous VAR," shows the worst that can happen at any point within a given investment horizon. Kritzman thus effectively questions the idea that investors should be willing to take more risk over longer horizons than shorter horizons by showing the actual amount of underestimation of VAR for several portfolios ranging from a long-only combination of half stocks and half bonds to a pairs trade. Then, using a simple mathematical model of relative importance, he shows that for relative volatility, when the correlation between both the securities and the asset classes is 50 percent, the choice of security is more important than the choice of asset class; only when the correlation of the securities is twice as high as the correlation of the asset classes does the asset allocation decision become more important. To finally settle the question of asset allocation versus security selection, Kritzman turns to bootstrapping, which allows for isolating the impact of security selection on the return distribution of many well-diversified portfolios. Even on a risk-adjusted basis, he affirms that the stock-selection decision is much more important than the asset allocation decision because it has much greater potential to influence wealth or happiness (utility).

Conclusion

The abilities required for comprehensive, coherent, well-articulated portfolio management are extraordinary and increasing. Portfolio managers must operate in the present but forecast the future and interpret the past. Portfolio managers can do many things to improve performance and clarify expectations; however, no one manager can do all of them at once. How to choose? Perhaps managers should heed the advice of fitness guru Covert Bailey, who answers the question of which exercises are best with this pithy response: "Whichever ones you will do every day."

Views of an "Informed" Trader

Harold S. Bradley
Senior Vice President
American Century Investment Management
Kansas City, Missouri

> The traditional and customary practices of order execution, including the use of soft dollars, are too often in conflict with achieving best execution for investors. Thus, these practices have come under scrutiny by the U.S. SEC and industry standard setters (such as AIMR), and firms have come under pressure to increase trade transparency and improve record keeping and accountability. Among the steps firms should take in this new environment is to demonstrate dedication to reducing trading costs, and among the best tools for that purpose (despite what many in the industry believe) is the electronic communication network.

As a former trader and portfolio manager at American Century Investment Management (ACIM), I have observed firsthand the difficulties involved in trading and the achievement of best execution. In particular, I have noticed how much of the investment management business uses the trading desk as a bill-paying function to support the business enterprise rather than as a mechanism for carrying out the fiduciary obligations owed to the client to provide best execution and to maximize the value of investment decisions. In this presentation, I will discuss the problems that stem from the myriad cross-subsidies that have been built into the commission stream and discuss how the current research payment systems may be subject to regulatory scrutiny and reform.

What Is Best Execution?

A definition of best execution appears just about everywhere: due diligence manuals, marketing presentations, consultant questionnaires, and requests for proposals. No legal definition exists, however, or at least traditionally, there has not been one. Thus, the search for best execution has proven elusive, despite the many assurances otherwise. "We know it when we see it, but it is really hard to measure," is an oft-quoted expression on trading desks when alluding to the concept of best execution. Traders are not paid to make decisions that really work to achieve best execution and have disincentives to doing so: They have soft dollar chits to pay and shares waiting to trade for impatient, demanding, and often unrealistic portfolio managers. Traders operate under what I call "maximum risk aversion for maximum pay on the desk." As a portfolio manager, when I made a bad decision, I blamed the trading desk. Trading is a function in which it is difficult to claim "value added" and easy to look bad in a handful of trades. As a result, it is no surprise that traders give the ambivalent answers they do when asked about best execution.

New Definition. In 2000, before leaving the U.S. SEC, former commissioner Arthur Levitt started the process of articulating new standards for best execution. At the same time, both the Investment Company Institute (ICI) and AIMR were asked to convene best practices groups to help define best execution. At the December 2000 ICI Securities Law Development Conference, Gene Gohlke, associate director of the SEC Office of Compliance Inspections and Examinations, offered this definition of best execution:

> In placing a trade, the trading desk will seek to find a broker/dealer or alternative trading system that will execute a trade in a way that the trader believes will realize the maximum value of the investment decision.

Editor's note: This presentation is reprinted from the AIMR proceedings *Organizational Challenges for Investment Firms* (Charlottesville, VA: AIMR, May 2002).

Given the conventional wisdom surrounding best execution, this definition presents a challenge to the industry.

The "investment decision" referred to in Gohlke's definition pertains to the particular trade being executed—not to Goldman Sachs' research yesterday, First Boston's research last week, or a consultant who directs a lot of business to the firm. In terms of words, the change is minor, but in terms of policy, the change is rather substantial. And the addition of "alternative trading systems" in the definition is a big change. The use of electronic communication networks (ECNs) and nontraditional trading systems has exploded in the market in the past 10 years. Yet, I am told that on the buy side, institutional money managers still directly use these systems less than 7–8 percent of the time.

In his presentation at the ICI Conference, Gohlke identified possible areas in which SEC auditors will spend more time. Note that he was not talking to investment professionals but, rather, to the lawyers who advise the outside directors who, in turn, advise funds and money managers. Investment managers have fiduciary obligations to boards as well as to investors in the areas of compliance systems, compliance evaluation procedures, and record keeping. Accordingly, the SEC is saying that the hiring of a consultant to measure execution quality is not sufficient proof that a manager is in compliance with getting best execution; the adequacy of order-handling systems, trade-error experience, and timeliness of execution reports will be reviewed; and the allotment of initial public offering (IPO) shares against requested allocations will be assessed.

Basically, the SEC appears to have serious concerns about how Section 28(e) of the Securities Exchange Act of 1934, which provides a "safe harbor" for firms to pay up for research, has been used and interpreted. In addition, the use of ECNs—as venues that provide greater liquidity, price improvement, and lower commission rates—will be evaluated. Many people on the buy side are not using ECNs, and this new mandate from the SEC means that the regulators want to know why.

AIMR Trade Management Guidelines. AIMR's proposed Trade Management Guidelines on best execution were announced in November 2001.[1] The AIMR recommendations are consistent with the direction of the SEC. The guidelines recommend the establishment of trade management oversight committees that will be responsible for developing a trade management policy and a process to manage the efficacy of trades. Are you getting what you are paying for? Are you evaluating the service you received? And are you evaluating the providers of that service?

Specifically, the implications of these guidelines are as follows:

- Substantial infrastructure spending will occur to build record-keeping and reporting systems to track and audit trading information appropriately because so many firms still operate with inadequate order management systems.
- The negotiation of acceptable commission ranges and documentation of the variance between negotiated and actual commission rates will become necessary. Commission rates that held at 5–6 cents a share for more than a decade should and will be negotiated down to a level closer to the 1.00–1.25 cents a share rate paid on ECNs for execution-only services.
- Trade management oversight committees will be established, and the internal documents prepared for these committees will be auditable by the SEC. The SEC has already been asking for these materials.
- Real and potential conflicts of interest must be documented.
- The choice of a particular trading system must be supported, and the review and evaluation of trades, broker selection, and execution performance can be expected.

What Are Soft Dollars Really Buying?

In Gohlke's definition of best execution, traders are charged with maximizing the value of the trade decision. But Robert Schwartz, the Marvin M. Speiser Professor of Finance at Baruch College, City University of New York, and Benn Steil, at the Council of Foreign Investors, have studied how little control traders actually have over the execution decision. They sent questionnaires to the chief investment officers of major investment companies that asked, "Who at your firm controls institutional commission payments?" They found that 62 percent of all trades are not controlled by traders.[2] (This finding is consistent with my experience as a trader and portfolio manager.) The report also addresses how often commissions are used to pay for things other than best execution. And Steil, aggregating the information from a variety of reports on commission bundling, has stated that nearly two-thirds of soft dollar agree-

---

[1] The proposed guidelines are available at www.aimr.org/pdf/standards/proposed_tmg.pdf, and the final guidelines are expected to be issued in November 2002.

[2] Robert Schwartz and Benn Steil, "Controlling Institutional Trading Costs," *Journal of Portfolio Management* (Spring 2002):39–49.

ments are unwritten and more than one-third of brokers are a party to illegal soft dollar arrangements.[3]

Clearly, soft dollar agreements play an important role in the execution decision and are often in direct conflict with an investment firm's fiduciary duty to the client. What are soft dollars really buying? How extensively is soft dollar business affecting the trading decision and ultimately usurping the goal of best execution?

Research. Investment managers pay up for execution and have a safe harbor to do so to some extent under Section 28(e), because in exchange for paying up, they receive company proprietary research services, including access to analysts and road shows with corporate executives. But now that these executives are subject to Regulation Fair Disclosure (FD), why are managers still willing to pay up?

The willingness to pay up is especially thought-provoking because most investment management firms choose to "buy" their research from brand-name companies (paying up relatively more), even when firm or brand name is obviously not a proxy for quality. Based on the following observations, this attraction to brand appears to be quite misplaced: Only 41 percent of analysts at the 10 largest brokers (what I consider the brand-name brokers) rank as StarMine four- or five-star analysts, compared with 35 percent of analysts at all firms having 10 or more analysts.[4] Rankings are based on the earliest directional correctness and accuracy of the analysts' EPS estimates for the trailing four quarters and two years as well as on the accuracy of buy, sell, and hold recommendations. The top five firms with the largest percentage of four- and five-star analysts are regional or niche research firms without significant investment banking activities, namely, Buckingham Research Group, Gerard Klauer Mattison, Pacific Growth Equities, U.S. Bancorp, and WR Hambrecht + Company. At the 10 largest brokers, 25 percent of the analysts ranked poorly, as one- or two-star performers. Obviously, the rationale that brand-name research is a worthy use of the client's commission dollar is suspect at best. Yet, the industry persists in supporting the practice of "buying" research with soft dollars, which is a major factor in holding negotiated commission rates at the 6 cent level.

■ *A safe harbor?* In his speech to the Securities Industry Association in November 2000, Levitt asked whether portfolio managers were bringing to bear the pressure they should on brokerage commission rates and why the emergence of electronic markets had not driven full-service commissions lower. If a trade on an ECN costs a penny or less a share, why do most people on the buy side still pay 5–6 cents a share? Do portfolio managers and independent directors think 6 cents is safe, that it falls within the safe harbor exception of Section 28(e)?

Levitt said that 6 cents is not a safe rate and that those who think it is should reexamine the part of their business that is predicated on 6 cents being safe. The status quo of the industry's trading and execution practices is being seriously challenged by the SEC. And **Figure 1** shows that, although the median commission rate has been steadily decreasing since 1989 because of technological advances and commission unbundling, immediately following Levitt's speech in 2000, the median rate dropped below 5 cents a share. Apparently, the market heard and understood the message.

■ *The real cost of research.* Understandably, investors must pay a cost for block trading, capital facilitation, value-added research, and IPOs, but what is that cost (i.e., the real cost of trading)? **Figure 2** compares average cost-per-share rates at ACIM with the industry median. The solid dark line depicts the rates our agency brokers have been willing to negotiate. The rate has not dropped significantly since 1989, even though we have tried, with minimal success, to move it lower. (Of course, with regulators and professional organizations such as AIMR and ICI moving the issues of best execution and soft dollar business to the forefront, the tenor and tone of the market changed markedly in 2001.)

The dashed line in Figure 2 shows ACIM's average cost for using ECNs, where we do 35–40 percent of our business. The difference in the rate charged by our agency brokers and the rate charged by the ECNs can be thought of as a premium paid for research. In 2001, this premium was at an all-time high. When the value of research should be worth far less than ever before, given Regulation FD and the information overload via the Internet, the cost of soft dollar research is at a record high mainly because technology has lowered the *real* cost of trading while the "old rules" of trading and execution have kept the actual cost of trading artificially high.

I used to be convinced that the more business we did on ECNs, the more our costs would rise (and the less the marginal benefit would be) because of a structural reversion to the mean. **Table 1** illustrates, however, that the mean for all-in trading costs is down, not up. As our business on these nontraditional systems increases, our overall efficacy, as measured against other brokers doing similar business in

---

[3] Benn Steil, "Can Best Execution Be Achieved in the Current Market Structure?" Presentation given at the AIMR conference "Improving Portfolio Performance through Best Execution," November 30–December 1, 2000, Chicago.
[4] StarMine is an ACIM portfolio company.

Figure 1. NYSE-Listed Share Trading Volume and Capital Research Associates' (CRA's) Industry Median Commissions, 1989–2001

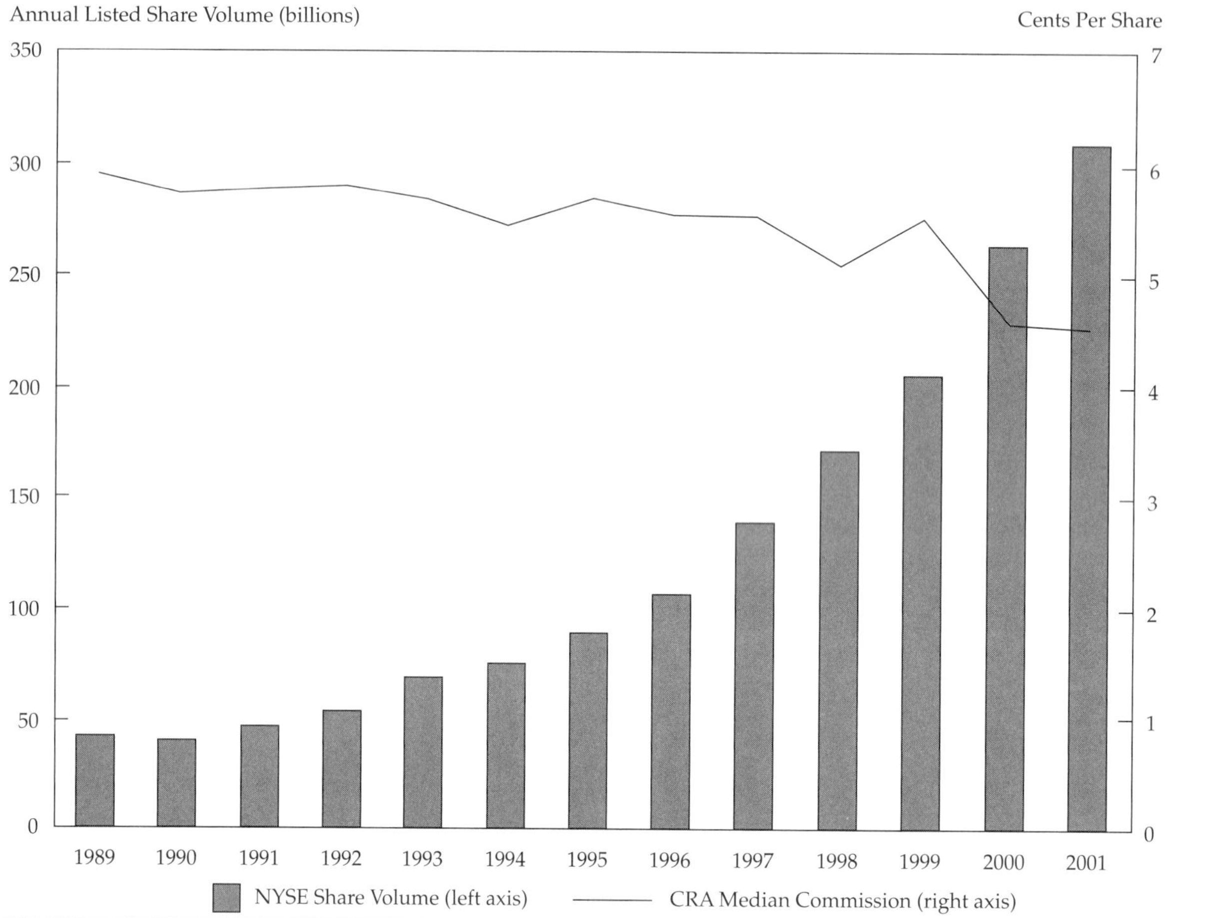

Note: Commission chart inclusive of ECN agency fees.

the same time frame, has widened. ECNs are far more effective than the traditional exchanges. They remove structural, intermediated costs.

The nontraditional players, highlighted in bold in Table 1, are important; in particular, B-Trade, Archipelago, and Instinet have helped lower our costs of trading. Broker 3, one of the most respected Nasdaq market-making firms in the business, produced costs equal to 2.03 percent of principal, round-trip, on Nasdaq trades, whereas Archipelago and Instinet both produced a negative cost. According to Capital Research Associates' methodology, "negative cost" means that the day after our order is finished, the price of the stock we sold is still falling. In other words, we have not telegraphed our intentions to the rest of the market in moving big orders, and we have succeeded in executing at a relatively fair price.

Use of electronic trading for listed stocks has only recently begun to pick up steam; Archipelago linked into the Nasdaq system to display orders in the public market early in 2001. Traders can now put their order indications into the public quote system and split the spreads charged by the specialists. The ability to lower costs this way is compelling.

Market Stability. For decades, brokers have justified all types of structural cross-subsidies by claiming that when markets are under stress, the broker will help stabilize the market. The popular theory was that the ability to get best execution depends on a broker's willingness to lay capital on the line during times of market distress, when that capital infusion is really needed.

In their article, Schwartz and Steil conclude, instead, that the buy-side institutions' call on street capital for immediacy of execution is an insurance or option to protect the investment manager's identity and order size from being captured by intermediaries and transmitted to competitors—to avoid being front-run. To support their contention, Schwartz and Steil point out that, based on the responses to their

Figure 2. Historical Commission Trends, 1989–2001

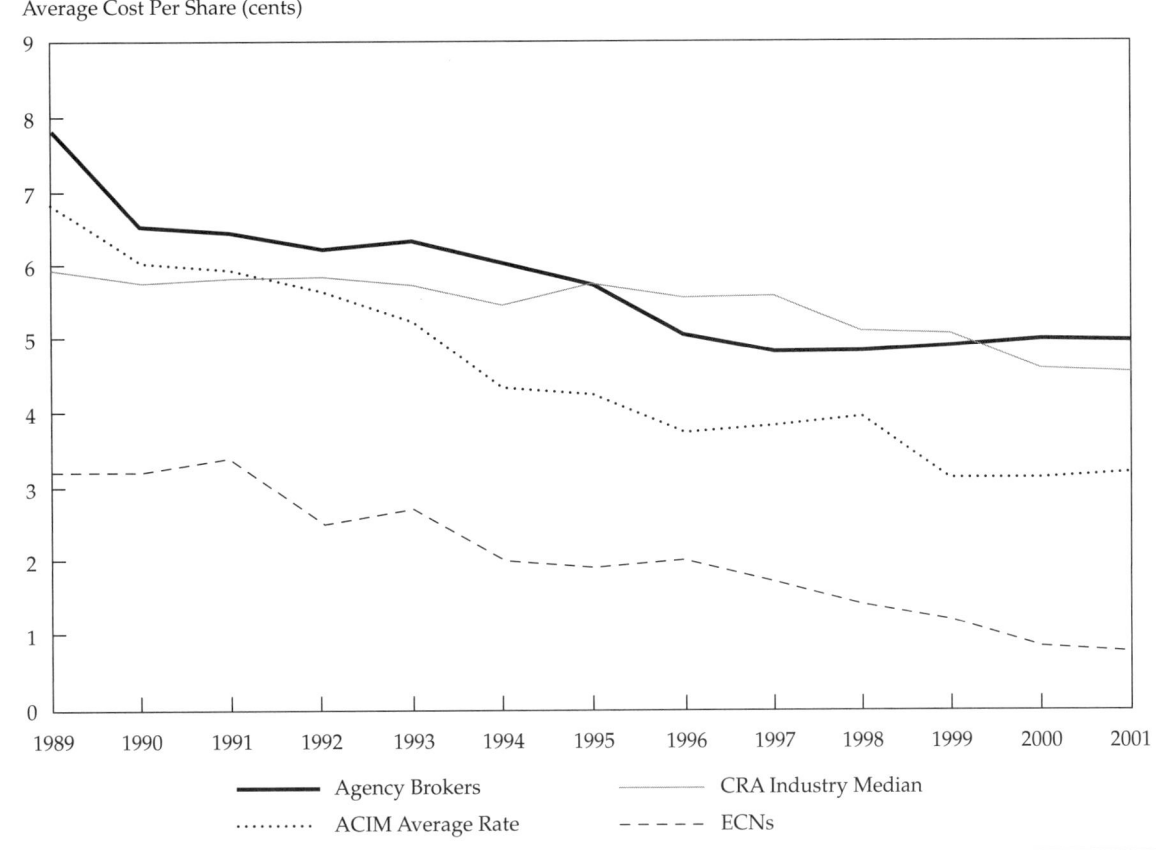

Table 1. Capital Research Associates' Study of ACIM All-In Trading Costs

Broker	Dollars Traded	Average Market Cap (billions)	Average Volatility	Cost as Percentage of Principal OTC	Cost as Percentage of Principal Listed
ACIM funds average	$47,607,820,875	$56.76	51%	0.49 bps	0.32 bps
Broker 1	4,263,056,375	48.67	45	0.66	0.28
Broker 2	2,637,630,000	47.28	45	0.93	0.23
Broker 3	1,672,943,750	42.69	56	2.03	–0.40
Broker 4[a]	1,738,325,000	35.23	51	–1.00	0.24
Instinet	2,219,195,000	61.35	61	–0.23	–2.72
Crossing Network	923,983,750	45.17	53	0.61	–0.25
B-Trade	3,697,211,250	56.24	63	0.84	–0.28
Archipelago	5,855,745,250	65.83	64	–0.06	–0.46
Traditional brokers[b]	10,311,955,125	43.47	49	0.66	0.09
Electronic brokers	12,696,135,250	57.15	60	0.29	–0.93

Note: Data reflect non-dollar-weighted mean of 10 six-month periods, June 30, 1997, through June 30, 2001 (post-order-handling rules).

[a]Negative OTC costs are a function of aftermarket IPO performance.
[b]The "traditional brokers" category reflects four large brokers only.

survey, portfolio managers only rarely create orders based on seeing the other side through a telephone call, trading activity, or order flow in the market. Investment managers appear to be attributing their willingness to pay up for liquidity to a reason that is not borne out in practice.

Order Life Cycle

Understanding how orders are executed and how the trading system is changing can shed light on the challenges of achieving best execution because of competing interests in the trading process. The life cycle of an order at the NYSE follows a convoluted route littered with at least seven intermediaries: An order travels from a portfolio manager to the trader; to a broker sales trader; to a "block," "position," or "upstairs" trader; to a floor broker; and finally, to the specialist post. Here is how it works. A portfolio manager decides to buy a stock and calls his institutional trader at the trading desk. That trader then tries to figure out which broker she might have heard from in the last two days that might have an order in that stock or, as likely, identifies a broker to whom the manager owes a consultant bill or who holds a soft dollar chit. She then gives the trade to the trader at that brokerage firm. The broker sales trader is the most frequent and trusted point of contact for the institutional sales trader.

But then there is the broker "upstairs" trader, whose job is to trade the firm's block capital. The reason brokers staff a sales trader position is ostensibly to protect the investor from the upstairs trader. For example, if the investor gives a 500,000-share order to the sales trader in Chicago, a trusted sales trader will not immediately disclose this information to the upstairs trader in New York. If the upstairs trader communicates this information throughout the system and is then asked to bid someone else's stock, that information alone might trigger "go along" activity and have an unfavorable impact on the price of the first trader's order. Investors need protection from the upstairs trader, but that upstairs trader is also the broker's representative for the investor's interest with the NYSE floor broker. The floor broker may be representing not only the firm representing that investor but also other firms and, therefore, other investors. The floor broker then goes to the specialist, who posts the order to the tape as part of the National Best Bid and Offer (NBBO) system, as seen on Bloomberg. The whole process is repeated on the other side of the trade.

Now consider order half-life. Orders travel from investor to specialist, with successively smaller order amounts passing from trader to trader within this sort of "bucket brigade." Everybody buys and sells exactly the same way. After an investor gives the institutional trader 500,000 shares to trade, that institutional trader gives the sales trader 250,000 shares to trade. The sales trader gives the upstairs trader 125,000 shares to trade, and the upstairs trader, through the floor broker, tells the specialist to post 25,000 shares. With such a system, no wonder traders believe that trading is a win–lose function.

In a market driven by eighths (before decimalization), commissions and trading spreads were plentiful and the mix of traditional roles in the execution process was sufficient assurance that everyone on the sell side would do well. In a market now driven by decimals, the life cycle of an order has not changed but the economics of the business certainly has. In the retail universe, a theory exists that payment for order flow and internalization of orders has been a large part of the profits of the business. This precedent is collapsing because both ECNs and decimalization have so markedly changed the economics of the execution process.

The Specialist. Because of the completely counterintuitive auction rules that govern trading on the NYSE, getting the best price in the market is often difficult. Let me explain what I mean with the following example. Say I go to a wine auction to buy a special case of wine. I want this wine badly because it is rated as one of the top wines of the new vintages; in 10 years, it will be worth a bundle, plus I will have good wine in the cellar. The bidding starts and quickly rises to $3,000 a bottle. I know I should not pay that much, but the auctioneer calls the bid and says I just purchased the wine. The case is opened, and I am handed four bottles—and then four bottles go to a person who was sitting three feet away from me who never opened her mouth, and another four bottles go to someone on the telephone. Before the bidding started and unknown to me, these two people said that they wanted to participate in the trade and buy at the highest price that cleared the supply.

Such are the rules of trading at the NYSE. The rules allow free options to third parties, so despite the theory published in the academic literature on auction markets, serious obstacles exist to discovering an appropriate clearing price. As long as a third party is allowed to forgo the risk of price discovery, that third party gets a free option on whatever is being traded. I find that situation fundamentally wrong. In my earlier example, the wine seller did not get the right price because I, as an interested buyer, was not allowed to bid for all the bottles I wanted and the other bidders were essentially removed from the bidding process altogether.

Little information is available on the profitability of specialists. A major NYSE specialist firm, LaBranche & Company, did recently go public, however, which provided some clues. The initial offering prospectus showed that LaBranche consistently earned more than 75 percent of its profits from dealer trader activity, had been profitable every quarter for 22 years, and averaged consistent returns on capital and equity of more than 70 percent. If LaBranche's numbers are typical of the economics of NYSE specialists, are investors benefiting from the intervention of the specialist, or do specialists simply impose another layer of expense?

Clean Cross Rule. The clean cross rule (Rule 72[b]) at the NYSE also grants a free option for liquidity takers and proprietary interests. A clean cross is a trade involving a matched pair of buy and sell orders of 25,000 shares or more that cannot be broken up (that is, disclosed floor interest is not included in the trade). Rule 72(b) currently gives priority to clean crosses at or within the prevailing quotation, and crosses are not allowed if any part of the cross is an order for the account of a member or member firm. An amendment to Rule 72(b) filed by the NYSE provides for clean crosses even if all or part of the order is for a member or member firm. Say you are a buyer bidding for 25,000 shares at $20 and the order is on the book as a limit order displayed for the whole world to see on Bloomberg. A broker has a customer who wants to sell 100,000 shares at $20 and another customer (or the broker himself) who wants to buy 100,000 at $20. They trade with each other, and your order remains unexecuted. Such a situation is worse than the situation with the specialist I just described because under the amendment, a broker can trade proprietarily on one side of a block trade and ignore preexisting orders on the trading floor.

The rules of trading are designed for the intermediaries and grant absolute free options to limit order traders in the market. Transparent limit orders provide the basis for price discovery in listed equities markets. I believe limit orders are an endangered species.

Institutional Xpress. The NYSE has finally paid attention to the ICI, which has been saying for a long time that limit orders are being subjected to free options. Accordingly, the NYSE established Institutional Xpress, which is designed to allow the institutional investor to take an offering or hit a displayed limit order through the NYSE DOT (designated order turnaround) system without an attempt to gain price improvement. Ironically, the rules governing Institutional Xpress provide an opportunity for, instead, price improvement of a market order. This is but another example of rules beneficial to brokers and inimical to the interests of buy-side traders.

Why *Not* ECNs?

ECNs improve the traditional execution mechanism and eliminate the requirement of dealing with the specialist. An ECN is a limit order book, and limit orders have primacy. The most important aspects of primacy are price priority, time priority, anonymity, and an order cancellation privilege—absolute control over entry into and exit from the market. The ability to cancel orders at will establishes a potential time value on options; they are no longer free. Nicholas Economides and Schwartz found that investors appreciate the motives for trading on ECNs but that the soft dollar arrangements that traders must satisfy may stymie ECN use.[5]

Nevertheless, despite the electronic trading systems' proven advantages, the buy side still has not welcomed ECNs with open arms. Ian Domowitz and Steil concluded:

> An examination of total trading costs, inclusive of commissions, reveals electronic trading to be superior to traditional brokerage by any measure of trade difficulty for buy trades and to be comparable for sells.[6]

Traders give several reasons for not trading on ECNs. Traders claim that large orders cannot be executed efficiently on ECNs and that executing through ECNs conflicts with the immediacy required to execute before an anticipated market move. Traders need to recognize that, in fact, ECNs not only offer the anonymity they seek but can also effectively execute large orders through rapid-fire, small, block-equivalent trades—as do brokers and market makers today.

Anonymity. Above all, both buy-side *and* sell-side traders seek order anonymity in the market. Yet, the identity of the firm, the size of the firm, and its trading practices are all known by the intermediary chosen to execute an order for a buy-side client. That intermediary has a relationship with at least 200 other high-commission-paying firms. Certainly, a relationship with some degree of trust exists between the trader and the sales trader, but that trust can break down rather easily. Because of the very nature of the

---
[5] Nicholas Economides and Robert A. Schwartz, "Equity Trading Practices and Market Structure: Assessing Asset Managers' Demand for Immediacy," *Financial Markets, Institutions & Instruments* (November 1995):1–45.

[6] Ian Domowitz and Benn Steil, "Automation, Trading Costs, and the Structure of the Securities Trading Industry," *Brookings-Wharton: Papers on Financial Services*, edited by Robert E. Litan and Anthony M. Santomero (Washington, DC: The Brookings Institution, 1999):33–81.

system, then, believing that a firm is working just for you or not leaking information about your order into the system is naive. ECNs, however, are the very definition of anonymity in trading.

Size. Traders have been heard to say, "Look at these screens. The orders are all for 1,000 shares, and on Nasdaq, they are offering 100 shares; there is no liquidity." This liquidity argument is largely moot; large, hidden limit orders, which are basically reserve quantities, exist on ECNs. The Nasdaq has just petitioned for a rule change that would allow market makers to show only 100 shares of an order to the market while at the same time placing as much as tens of thousands of shares in a nontransparent order queue. A benefit of this capability is that to trade 1,000 shares, you can execute 10 trades of 100 shares electronically and virtually simultaneously without advertising to adversaries what you are doing.

Buy-side traders prefer to trade large blocks of stock because blocks are easier to account for and to book. The typical trader's viewpoint is that block trades cannot be executed on ECNs. But we find that when we use an ECN for listed trades and an order is published and highly visible, we tend to attract the other side of an order more easily. That advantage has interesting implications, especially considering the recent merger between Archipelago and REDI-Book and the SEC's approval of Archipelago becoming a fully electronic exchange. With the emergence of a fully electronic exchange, the buy side will apparently be able to drive the best price in the market while avoiding unnecessary intermediation.

A block trade that uses a broker's capital is not a charitable gift. Brokers traditionally "rent" capital when trading a block because natural counterparties are said to occur only about 20 percent of the time. Brokers regularly make capital for block facilitation available only to payers of the largest commissions—which is functionally identical to offering a commission discount. Then, if they lose money on the trades, they earn full "rents" from smaller full-commission players, so they are making up the difference with commissions from the smaller firms that do not have that same kind of leverage with the broker. This "loss ratio" is a major component of the cross-subsidies that underpin the soft dollar business. Ultimately, the little guy loses.

Historically, brokers served as "small order aggregators" working off negotiated block transactions in small increments over the phone, SelectNet, or ECNs. ECNs, however, eliminate the risk premium that institutions pay to trade; technology replaces capital in the aggregation process.

Our traders work aggressively to get the best price for block size on ECNs. At ACIM, we use FIX technology, the financial information exchange protocol, to send orders to ECNs, and we have been successful in trading extremely large orders on ECNs; we regularly execute orders of more than a million shares. Surprisingly, the average trade size for a Nasdaq stock on an ECN is fewer than 1,000 shares. We use DOT and Archipelago to access the liquidity on the NYSE, and we are increasingly successful at trading large orders in NYSE-listed securities on ECNs.

A good example of our success in trading blocks on ECNs is what we were able to accomplish during the period from June 1 to August 31, 2001, the summer doldrums, when the entire equity market's volume is at its lowest level. We averaged on a daily basis more than 13 orders of more than 50,000 shares; 6 orders between 50,000 and 100,000 shares; 4 orders between 101,000 and 250,000 shares; and almost 2 orders between 251,000 and 500,000 shares. And these trade sizes are fairly conservative in terms of what can be executed on ECNs. For example, during the same period, we used ECNs to trade 12.1 million shares of AOL with an average order size of 202,000 shares and a total principal value of $526 million. We also traded 12.1 million shares of Pfizer ($494 million of principal and average order size of 181,000 shares).

We chose to make these trades on ECNs because we wanted anonymity. When the market sees you trading in a name, the other buyers immediately look to see how big you are in the name and make inferences about why you are selling or buying. That is how the Street anticipates price action.

Immediacy. Another buy-side trader objection to using ECNs is the need to implement a trade "right now" in one block at a single price. Part of the trader's demand for immediacy is the culture of blame transfer—that is, portfolio managers blaming traders for the portfolio managers' own mistakes. When the buy-side trader hands an order to a broker, the trader has someone to yell at on behalf of an impatient portfolio manager.

Schwartz and Steil surveyed portfolio managers and chief investment officers about how much weight they give in stock purchase decisions to an estimate of share price in one day, one week, one quarter, one year, and two years or more. Most managers profess that they do not care what the share price will be one day or even one quarter out but do care about the price at one to two years out. That finding has profound implications. Why would portfolio managers, who may take days or weeks to make a purchase or sell decision, expect a trade to be done "right now" unless their ego is heavily invested in micromanaging the trader? Schwartz and Steil also asked how soon the managers expected a price correction to occur when buying or selling a stock that was believed to be mispriced. Most answered one month to one year or more than one year, not less than an hour or one week to one month. So, again, managers' timing expectations do not appear to align with their demands. Immediacy is simply not the impetus for trading that many managers claim.

Changes Affecting ECNs

In 1975, the Exchange Act called for a linked national market in which prices in one market would be respected in other markets. More than 20 years passed before the SEC took another major step toward encouraging market linkage with the enactment of the order-handling rules in 1997. These rules were an attempt to tie together markets fragmented by Instinet and other ECNs. It required ECNs to include orders in the public display of the NBBO. Although the Nasdaq intermarket gives ECNs a path to the listed market and exchange-traded funds, barriers to unification of the markets exist, such as the access fee the ECNs are charged. Archipelago chose to voluntarily comply with the order-handling rules but is the only ECN to have done so. The SEC has suggested that the application of the order-handling rules and Regulation ATS (alternative trading systems) to listed stocks is unfinished business. ECNs, however, represent an estimated 40 percent of Nasdaq volume, and ECN quotes drive the inside market.

The intermarket trading system (ITS)/Computer Assisted Execution System (CAES) link to the NBBO offered by Nasdaq to its members, who include Archipelago, is rapidly changing the marketplace. For the 62 days ending March 31, 2001, before Archipelago linked to the market through ITS/CAES, we traded only 35 orders for NYSE-listed stocks, compared with 121 listed orders in the 65 days after the linkage on August 31, 2001. Pre-ITS/CAES, these orders were excluded from market quotes, but post-ITS/CAES, the orders were transparent as limit orders to all market participants. We can now advertise our intention to trade.

Nevertheless, some traders are expressing frustrations similar to those expressed about Nasdaq trades before the instigation of the order-handling rules. The complaint is about "trade-throughs" and "backing away" (the latter occurs when one linked market trades at an inferior price to another market's price—say, the NYSE— as reflected in the NBBO). We started putting our listed orders into the system, and because of trade-throughs, we could not get some trades executed without compromise. As a result, Archipelago and Nasdaq built so-called whiner software (because we whined a lot). The "whine" is automatically triggered when (1) the public quote exceeds 100 shares at a price in the NBBO and (2) the order in Archipelago's ARCA book is at a superior price to the competing exchange and (3) the ARCA order is displayed for 15 seconds before a trade takes place at the inferior price in the NYSE and (4) the trade remains unexecuted for at least 10 seconds after the trade at the inferior price.

Whining is a frequent occurrence. The specialists believe the market resides with them, and an imputed belief is that the regional exchanges are not contributing to price discovery, which has, in fact, been true historically. Prior to decimalization, the regional exchanges were used primarily by retail firms, such as Charles Schwab & Company, to maximize profitability by routing orders and earning payment for order flow from the regional exchanges.

Since decimalization, the practice of payment for order flow appears to be breaking down, which has changed the economic structure of many order flow arrangements. Now, as real electronic orders flow through Nasdaq (and, soon, through the Pacific Coast Exchange), the NYSE is trying to make sure orders have to come to it. A good audit trail does not exist that reveals the primary exchanges' failure to recognize better prices on regional exchanges. But from mid-June through August 2001, Archipelago and Nasdaq recorded more than 1,500 NYSE whines a day, which is a big concern. It means that either the specialists cannot keep up with both an electronic market and a physical market, which is a reasonable explanation, or that they are ignoring the electronic market because they are granting free options to the floor crowd.

Until the market adjusts to a more integrated system, these whines have important implications for how managers manage, especially given the environment of 2–4 percent real expected stock returns suggested by Robert Arnott and Peter Bernstein[7] and the fact that the cost of trading is estimated to be 1–3 percent for small- and mid-cap stocks.

The impediments to trading are regulatory— that is, driven by market regulations designed to protect the owners of the marketplace. I am a big fan of Archipelago's move to partner with the Pacific Stock Exchange to form a new for-profit stock exchange. A for-profit stock exchange is not owned by intermediaries and not run for intermediaries; it is owned by and run for the stockholders.

---

[7] Robert D. Arnott and Peter L. Bernstein, "What Risk Premium Is 'Normal'?" *Financial Analysts Journal* (March/April 2002):64–85.

Conclusion

The problems with achieving best execution cannot be separated from the existing economics of trading systems and the reluctance of traders and portfolio managers to change the way they approach the trading function. Roughly 65 percent of ECN users are broker/dealers and hedge funds and 25 percent are day traders. As I mentioned earlier, only about 7–8 percent of ECN users are on the buy side. Schwartz and Steil wrote:

> Survey results clearly suggest that the traditional explanation for immediacy demand . . . is overstated. We conclude that the buy side's demand for immediacy is in appreciable part endogenous to an intermediated environment that is characterized by front-running.

Although some may find this view to be too cynical, the statement summarizes the behavior and rationale that I have witnessed over the course of my career.

Is unbundling of commissions and research and other soft dollar services desirable and feasible? In the same Schwartz and Steil survey mentioned previously, they found that 51 percent of managers believe unbundling commissions from the research process is desirable and only 8 percent believe it is undesirable. The bundled process, however, has a major positive impact on the earnings stream of many investment managers.

In the United Kingdom, Paul Myners, chairman of the Gartmore Group and one of the most respected money managers in the United Kingdom, was asked to investigate the inefficiencies of capital formation for small- and mid-cap U.K. firms. One of the recommendations he made was that all commissions be paid by the manager out of the management fee. U.K. firms have been given two years to respond to and implement the recommendations.

Although such action is a long way off in the United States, in light of the SEC's direction and AIMR's new guidelines, U.S. firms should begin to address the following questions:

- Is the commission you pay really protected by the safe harbor? It probably is not safe at 6 cents, or even 5 cents.
- Do you use ECNs? When? How much? How do you make that choice? You must first give your traders permission to be traders.
- Do you pay the same brokerage rate to all vendors and the same rate on all trades? If so, why? Lower negotiated rates alone are not sufficient. The SEC is looking for some variance within the rates paid to the same broker among trades. Some firms are paying 2–3 cents for taking the other side of a trade and paying 6 cents for capital commitment. These investment management firms have a formula for determining what they pay for various kinds of trades.
- How do you measure best execution? Whether you use Capital Research Associates, Plexus Group (implementation shortfall methodology), or volume-weighted average price, part of the answer to achieving best execution lies in having a process to measure it.
- Have you invested in sufficient trading technology? Or are your traders bill-paying order clerks?
- Do you know where your orders go? The order execution process is, in my opinion, sausage making at its worst. It is where the source of performance resides, especially in a potentially low-return environment.
- Regarding step-outs, are the rates and best execution promises consistent with what your marketing agent tells the sponsor? A lot of firms use step-outs and think they are getting best execution by using them. But almost everybody I talk to on the sell side tells me they have an A list and a B list, and the firms that step out are on the B list. If you are calling a potential buyer with merchandise and you know there are three or four buyers around and you have a seller for something that is hot, you call the buyer that will maximize your income. You cannot maximize your income on that trade if 40 percent of the trade is going to be stepped out to a third party.

Attention to these issues will help firms get on the right track and avoid problems in the future.

The bottom line is that trading decisions are not driven simply by the search for best execution. Too many conflicting economic currents and motivations affect the execution decision, which more often than not is made by someone other than the trader. Paying up to execute is a function of the traditional and customary practice of buying broker services—research and market stability—with soft dollars, but this practice has been targeted by the SEC and industry standard setters (such as AIMR) as needing increased transparency and improved record keeping and accountability.

Question and Answer Session
Harold S. Bradley

Question: How do you measure trading costs when Elkins/McSherry, Plexus Group, and others are using "fuzzy math" to calculate the costs?

Bradley: Elkins/McSherry is the biggest consultant in the VWAP (volume-weighted average price) measurement service. Generally speaking, its study of VWAP simply says if your buys are under the VWAP, that's good, and if your sells are over, that's bad. I think the VWAP mechanism is flawed; in fact, it is influencing price discovery processes in the market, and some dealers have even structured trades so that they look good in that study. A trader trying to "game" this system would simply stop buying shares of a large order if the day's price exceeds the trade-weighted price for the day. Many vendors report this price throughout the day. At its logical extreme, a trade that might be done in one day is stretched over several days if the price continues to trade higher. Several years ago, we had one trade that looked wonderful on a VWAP basis but was actually the worst when measured with the Capital Research Associates (CRA) market impact study.

Having been a portfolio manager, I know that the Plexus function is also troublesome because of difficulties in effectively capturing data. Plexus bases its analyses on the Perold implementation shortfall methodology, which tries to measure the implementation cost from the time a portfolio manager has the original trade idea, through the time the trader gets the order, to the time the order is executed, including the opportunity cost of cancelled orders.[1] The problem with this methodology is that a portfolio manager often "sits" on an analyst's recommendation or idea for a couple of days (or even weeks) as the portfolio manager considers the analysis in a market context. The portfolio manager often does not act on the analyst's recommendation until the stock starts to move and it looks as though the analyst was right. That kind of behavior might handcuff a trader asked to join the crowd. When did the portfolio manager really get the idea on which the Perold methodology is predicated? That's a difficult data-gathering problem. What is a fair measure? Many traders I know think that there should be more science behind the ability to capture the information on the front end. For most firms, that is a major potential flaw in the methodology, as I understand it.

At American Century, we like the market impact methodology used by CRA, which uses Gil Beebower's method of looking at day-after performance as measured against the market and industry groups. This technique contains biases and flaws, as well. None of these methods is perfect. Simply put, Beebower's method says that if you buy a stock over a period of five days and tomorrow it decreases more than its industry group sector, you suffer a positive trading cost or market impact. If the stock goes up more than the market or sector on the day following completion of the trade, you get credit for "negative" trading costs.

Question: How does Beebower's method of measuring trading costs differ from the other methods?

Bradley: The Beebower methodology tries to quantify a "rubber-band" effect that often occurs, what in trader slang is called "window shading." Wall Street's sell-side traders talk about the "window shade" of principal block trades. Many buy-side traders are not even familiar with the term. Let me try and explain: I sell 100,000 shares of a million share order to a broker's principal bid as that broker "gets me started." The broker uses his capital on the first part of the order and then widely communicates to other buyers that "he's long and working a big seller." The market will trade down to a clearing price, at which point the broker's phone rings off the hook. A typical buy-side trader doesn't want to look bad and might leave the broker instructions to "call me when the seller doesn't have any more (sell orders) behind." A good principal trader at the block-trading houses assesses the latent demand and knows when to bid the seller for big size at a dislocated price. He effectively pulls the window shade down and buys the rest of the block, cleaning up the seller. Then, the window shade snaps back with a vengeance as buyers are left with unfilled orders. The sell-side brokers are making calls to let the formerly cautious and patient buyers know that the seller is gone and the market "looks better."

This ritual dance raises costs to both sellers and buyers. The buyers now panic because they missed the best prices (but, of course, they're still under the VWAP!). The broker may stay "long on his book" maybe 200,000 shares that he sells into recovering prices; that is the only way he can fight back to even with that first badly priced 100,000 shares. So, what Beebower measures is a longer-term window shade.

---

[1] André F. Perold, "The Implementation Shortfall: Paper vs. Reality," *Journal of Portfolio Management* (Spring 1988):4–9.

Again, I think that what happens in shorter time periods in the market also happens in longer time periods. Different ways to measure trading costs exist. Plexus and CRA at least use a standardized method across the industry, which allows a firm to evaluate its relative trading effectiveness. That is why we began using ECNs in the first place. The data were counterintuitive, but we simply kept pushing the envelope as long as the data supported it, and we eventually became rabid sponsors of these new efficient electronic trading approaches because the data suggested we were removing significant trading costs from both easy and difficult trades.

Question: What would you estimate the Street's costs for basic brokerage to be—a penny a share? Why not separate research from execution; that is, write a check for research and pay a penny a share for execution?

Bradley: The real cost of execution is the ECN rate, not the cost of a heavily human-intermediated function. The ECN rate has been under a penny a share for a year. The agency broker rate, or the fully bundled rate, has been about 5 cents a share, but this rate is on the verge of being undercut for the first time in more than a decade.

In fact, over the years, we have been made aware that some brokers who would not budge on 5-cent bundled rates for American Century shareholders and clients would provide our clients a 1 cent or 2 cent rebate as part of a commission recapture program. In effect, they are saying to my client that the real cost of an agency execution is only 3 cents or 4 cents per share. That makes me irate: You are going to do cheaper business for my customer, whom I am trying to manage money for, but you are not going to give me that same rate? That is because there are two different operating subsidiaries for these firms trying to do the same business. These subsidiaries are in a price war within their own firms. The spread between the execution-only rate assessed by ECNs and the bundled rate for research, execution, liquidity, and other services is the effective payment rate for research, which I argue is near a historical wide point—about 4.25 cents.

The question I have is whether research is of more value today than it was before Regulation FD and the advent of Web-based systems that allow for an infinite number of participants on a company's earnings release conference call. I believe that some research and access to specific research analysts may well be worth this 28(e) investment (the so-called safe harbor in federal securities legislation that allows for an investment firm to "pay up" for research that benefits a fund's shareholders). That is why I believe so strongly in what StarMine is trying to do. StarMine has created a four star system to evaluate which analysts in which stocks are courageous, right, and early. StarMine is attempting to provide a quality brand, and I am willing to pay for a product that is valuable.

Regarding the question of unbundling, the Street is afraid that they will not be paid enough. This concern has major implications for how firms structure and conduct business. I argue that there is value to be had, but you have to know how to find it. So, I am investing in such companies as StarMine to try to brand some of this research as valuable for investors who really think and are not afraid to be different from the crowd.

Question: Are ECNs effective on short sales?

Bradley: ECNs are awesome on short sales. ECNs have always allowed for trading in increments of 1/256th. So, even as people argued over decimals on the Nasdaq and NYSE, you could regularly trade in 64ths, 128ths, and 256ths on Instinet, Archipelago, Bloomberg, and other ECNs. A decimal is a fraction, after all; ECNs simply split the 8th to infinity.

Hedge funds have been big users of short-selling strategies on ECNs for a long time for this reason. When the market was a fixed-eighth market five years ago, a hedge fund could go into an ECN up 1/32nd or 1/64th and get off a short that was on an uptick, not recognized on the public tape. And by using smaller orders, I found that the efficacy of my short selling on the Nasdaq was far superior in terms of time of execution, percentage of fulfilled orders, and price impact than it was on the NYSE, where I had a much higher opportunity cost for unfilled orders and a much longer duration before execution.

Question: Do you expect the impact of Nasdaq's SuperMontage on ECNs to be positive or negative?

Bradley: A huge change is under way. I was invited to participate on a Federal Advisory Committee by Chairman Levitt before he left the SEC, and we looked at the pricing mechanisms for the exchanges. Not many people clearly understand regulatory funding mechanisms and the significant income that exchanges derive from sharing tape print revenues. For every trade printed on what is called the "consolidated tape," the exchanges get paid. When the plan for sharing tape print revenues was established in the late 1970s, it was intended to fund the exchanges' self-regulation costs. I am told that those "plans" have become a major source of exchange revenue and marketing budgets.

Recently, however, Island ECN, now the largest ECN, made a deal with the Cincinnati Stock Exchange; the exchange will share revenues with Island for all trades printed on the exchange. Also, Archipelago acts as a facility for the

Pacific Coast Stock Exchange (PCX) and is in the process of turning the exchange into a fully electronic exchange. Archipelago wants the regulatory status and the ability to be a member of "the club" that the exchange can bestow. By belonging to the club, Archipelago gains a share of tape revenues; so, every trade that gets printed on the PCX will bring in revenue for Archipelago.

When Island did its deal with the Cincinnati Stock Exchange, Island was one of Nasdaq's biggest customers. If Island is now going to print and show all its business through Cincinnati because of the revenue arrangement, that is about 20 percent of the daily trading volume of the Nasdaq stock market. Archipelago and REDI (who recently merged) represent a large percentage of the Nasdaq stock market trading volume, and Archipelago now is going to be doing the same thing on the PCX. Therefore, I see equalization and competition based on the "revenue and trade print revenue" screen. The details of this change may seem arcane and complicated, but the change is interesting because billions of dollars are at stake.

Question: Do brokerage firms take advantage of buy-side order flow? If so, how?

Bradley: Of course brokerage firms take advantage of buy-side order flow. They are intermediaries. Some firms take advantage of it proprietarily, but not all firms do. The real issue is how brokerage firms take care of their customers and what kind of customers they have. For example, floor constituents from the NYSE have asked me to try and bring attention to a large hedge fund and its relationship with Wall Street because they are convinced this fund pays as much as 15 cents a share simply to find out where big orders are from other customers. There are many different ways—with revenue streams that are opaque—to leverage and harness operating margin and relationships. That is why anonymity is so important.

How Much Diversification Is Enough?

Burton G. Malkiel
Chemical Bank Chairman's Professor of Economics
Princeton University
Princeton, New Jersey

> Achieving diversification in today's uncertain markets requires a reexamination of basic portfolio selection theory. Idiosyncratic risk is becoming more difficult to eliminate from portfolios, and the question of international diversification poses further challenges. To be adequately diversified, investors should hold a wide variety of common stocks and include nontraditional asset classes, namely, REITs (real estate investment trusts) and Treasury Inflation-Indexed Securities, in their portfolios. They should also consider making index funds a core component of their diversification strategy.

In this presentation, I will offer specific advice about portfolio construction. I will first address the question of how much diversification is enough given the volatility in today's market. I will then discuss the efficacy of international diversification and diversification into a wide array of asset classes: that is, real estate, bonds, and Treasury Inflation-Indexed Securities (formerly known as Treasury Inflation-Protected Securities or TIPS) have shown signs that they are currently particularly useful diversifiers. I will also emphasize the advantages of using indexing as a strategy to accomplish clients' investment objectives.

Idiosyncratic Risk and Portfolio Construction

According to one of the basic tenets of portfolio selection theory, even though market, or systematic, risk cannot be eliminated from a portfolio, company-specific, or idiosyncratic, risk can be diversified away. Recent changes in the market environment have challenged certain aspects of this theory and pose challenges for investors who aim to be adequately diversified.

Idiosyncratic Risk in Theory. I recently conducted a study with John Campbell and others in which we measured the volatility of individual stocks in different ways and looked at the variance in daily, monthly, and quarterly returns.[1] We analyzed how much idiosyncratic risk was present in the price movement of each stock. The first step was to measure the beta of each stock—the risk associated with a stock that cannot be diversified away. Idiosyncratic risk—the unique risk associated with a stock that can be diversified away—is the "fuzz" around the regression line that measures a stock's beta. In other words, together, idiosyncratic risk and beta equal a stock's total volatility.

Regardless of the method we used to measure individual company volatility, the result was a graph resembling the one illustrated in **Figure 1**, which shows that the volatility of individual stocks has unmistakably risen over time. Meanwhile, market volatility, which was very high following the crash of 1987 and has been slightly higher in the past few years, has been virtually trendless. The increased volatility in individual stocks is also obvious in the largest percentage point gainers and losers published in the *Wall Street Journal*. It used to be that the movement up or down was in the neighborhood of 10 percent, but it is now up or down 50 percent. Without a doubt, the volatility of individual stocks has risen, yet idiosyncratic risk, according to portfolio theory, is precisely the risk that diversification is supposed to eliminate.

---

[1] John Y. Campbell, Martin Lettau, Burton G. Malkiel, and Yexiao Xu, "Have Individual Stocks Become More Volatile? An Empirical Investigation of Idiosyncratic Risk," *Journal of Finance* (February 2001):1–44.

Figure 1. Individual Company Volatility, July 1962–December 1997

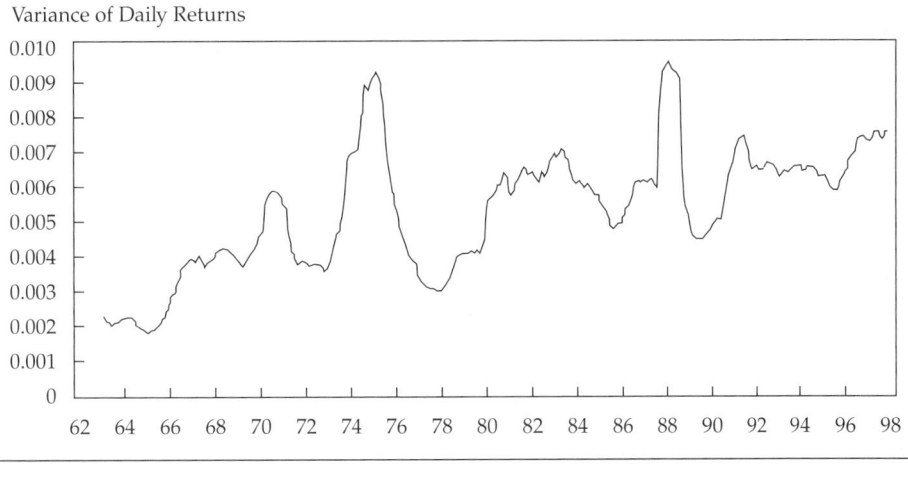

Idiosyncratic Risk in Practice. Figure 2 indicates why idiosyncratic risk matters in determining how much diversification is enough. The figure contrasts the diminishing level of total portfolio risk for two time periods (1960s and 1990s) as the portfolio grows from one security to 50 securities. The data presented by the solid line representing the situation in the 1960s, which can be found in any standard finance textbook, suggest the following. If a portfolio is formed from a universe of randomly selected stocks, all of which have a beta of around 1, the total portfolio risk in a one-stock portfolio in terms of variance of returns will be high because the portfolio will have not only systematic risk but also company-specific, or idiosyncratic, risk. In a 20-stock portfolio (as long as the stocks are diversified in terms of sector), idiosyncratic risk will effectively be diversified away and total portfolio risk will be the average beta of the portfolio (in this case a beta of 1), or at least that was the theory in the 1960s. Now, given that individual stocks are much more volatile, 20- and even 50-stock portfolios still contain a significant amount of idiosyncratic risk. To eliminate idiosyncratic risk in today's market, a portfolio must hold many more stocks than the 20 stocks that in the 1960s achieved sufficient diversification.

One way for an investor to achieve adequate diversification is to buy the entire market by buying a fund benchmarked to the Wilshire 5000 Index, which is composed of about 6,500 stocks. But whether or not this approach is followed, sufficient diversification to eliminate idiosyncratic risk now requires many more stocks than in the 1960s. The theory as it pertains to diversification and idiosyncratic risk in most older finance textbooks is no longer accurate.

International Stocks and Portfolio Construction

I will now examine the diversification benefits of adding international stocks to a domestic equity portfolio. As Bruno Solnik mentioned, this diversification strategy has its detractors.[2]

International Diversification in Theory. Simply put, adding asset classes other than domestic stocks to a diversified domestic equity portfolio can reduce total portfolio risk if the asset class added has a low correlation with the other stocks in the portfolio. The correlation coefficient falls between –1 and 1: +1 means that the prices of the two asset classes move entirely in lockstep; zero means that no relationship exists between the price movement of the two asset

Figure 2. Idiosyncratic Risk and Risk Reduction

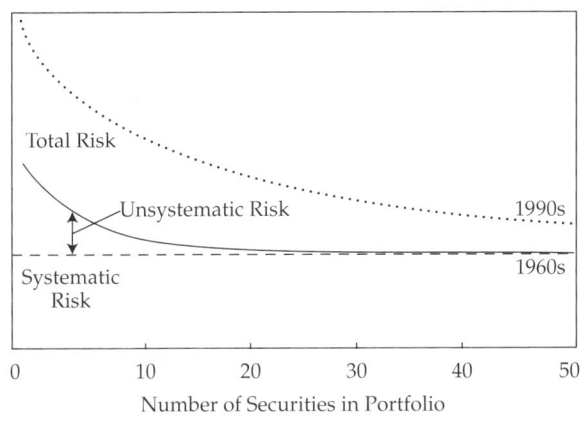

[2] See Professor Solnik's presentation in this proceedings.

classes; and −1 means that the assets are perfectly negatively correlated (when one market is up, the other is invariably down).

Figure 3 illustrates the correlation between two assets, say, a U.S. equity index fund (Asset 1) and an MSCI Europe/Australasia/Far East (EAFE) index fund (Asset 2). Risk in Figure 3 is measured by the standard deviation of returns. Asset 1 has a lower expected return with lower expected risk (a lower standard deviation) than Asset 2. If r, the correlation coefficient, is +1, then the prices of both assets will move in lockstep, in which case portfolio theory says that an investor will not get any risk reduction from diversification. If an investor has half of his or her assets in Asset 1 and half in Asset 2, he or she will get half the returns and half the risk of both, but no benefit, no lowering of total portfolio risk, will be derived from diversification. If, however, the correlation is −1, then some combination of the two assets will completely eliminate portfolio risk (by risk, I mean the standard deviation of the returns from period to period). If the correlation is positive but less than 1 (+0.3 in Figure 3), the two assets are positively, but not completely, correlated. In this case, some combination of the two assets, a decrease in Asset 1 and an increase in Asset 2, results in an increase in portfolio return and a reduction in portfolio risk. So, to the extent that an investor can add an asset class that is less than perfectly correlated with the basic asset class in his or her portfolio, this addition can reduce the portfolio's risk and increase its return. Harry Markowitz won the Nobel Prize in economics in 1990 for teaching investors this important lesson.

Figure 3. Correlation and Risk Reduction

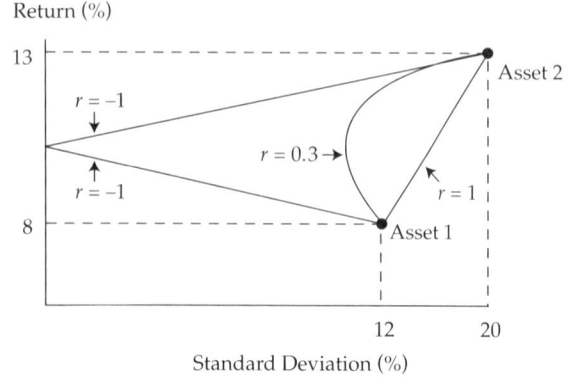

International Diversification in Practice.

Figure 4 shows different combinations of risk and return for an S&P 500 index fund (Asset 1) and an EAFE index fund (Asset 2) from 1970 to 1998. This figure reflects Bruno Solnik's earlier work, in which he documented the home-country bias and concluded that investors should diversify internationally.[3] His theory was borne out in practice: A portfolio composed of 25 percent EAFE stocks and 75 percent U.S. stocks produced a higher return with lower risk than a purely domestic U.S. portfolio during that time period. Finance textbooks present this theory as being the nearest thing to a free lunch that the financial markets offer investors. If this theory is true, however, then why is international diversification not more widely accepted in practice? Why, for instance, did French institutional investors hold 97 percent of their portfolios in French stocks prior to the adoption of the euro? Identifying the benefits of international diversification led to the classification of the phenomenon known as the "home-country bias puzzle" in the finance literature.

Figure 4. Diversification with U.S. and Other Developed Country Stocks, 1970–1998

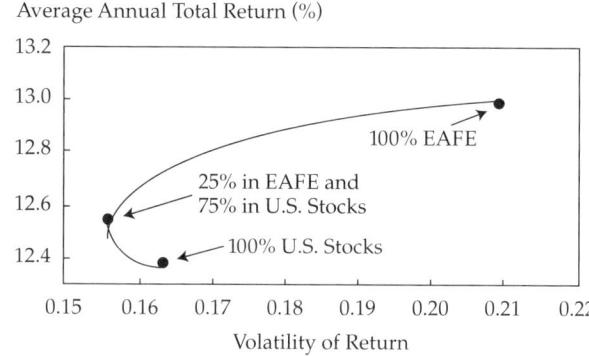

Note: Returns in U.S. dollars include capital gains and dividends.

Figure 5, which plots the rolling correlations of the S&P 500 Index/EAFE and the S&P 500/MSCI Emerging Markets Index for every quarter from 1988 to 2001, sheds light on why international diversification now has many skeptics. Since about 1997, the correlation between EAFE stocks and U.S. stocks has been rising. At the end of 2001, the correlation between U.S. and EAFE stocks was above 0.8, very close to +1, which is significantly higher than the correlation in earlier quarters over the period studied. Theory states that if the correlation of two asset classes is close to +1, combining the two asset classes in a single portfolio does not reduce total portfolio risk. Globalization has, without a doubt, caused the world's securities markets to move in a much more synchronized fashion. Figure 5 also shows that the

---
[3] Bruno H. Solnik, "The International Pricing of Risk: An Empirical Investigation of the World Capital Market Structure," *Journal of Finance* (May 1974):365–378.

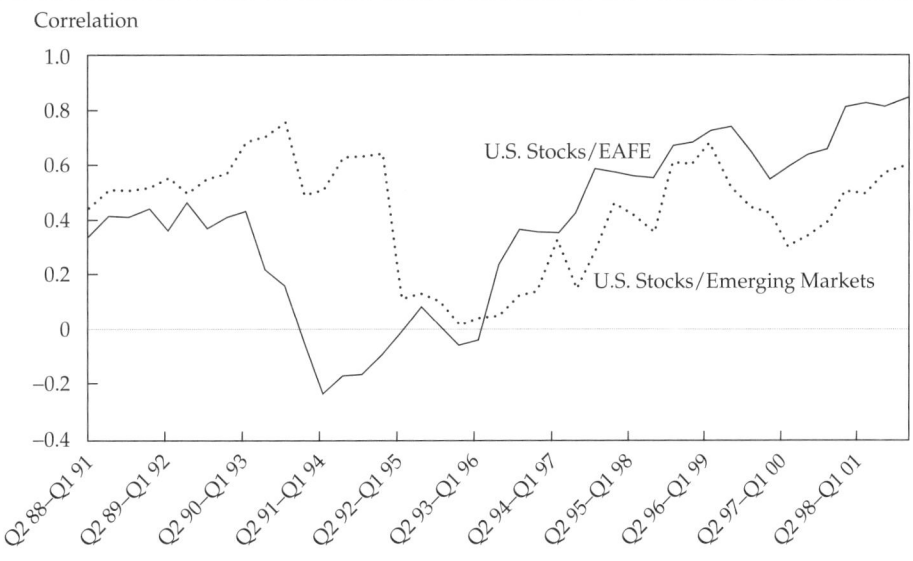

Figure 5. Quarterly Rolling Correlations: U.S./EAFE Stocks versus U.S./Emerging Market Stocks, June 1988–September 2001

correlation between U.S. stocks and emerging market stocks has varied over the 1988–2001 period, from a low of 0 to a high of just under 0.8. Since 1997, just as the correlation of U.S. stocks and EAFE stocks has increased, the correlation of U.S. stocks and emerging market stocks has increased from its most recent low of around 0.3 to around 0.6, but it still exhibits a lower correlation than U.S. stocks with EAFE stocks.

In addition to the fact that developed foreign markets are moving almost in lockstep with the U.S. market, critics of international diversification have a second argument. Not only is the correlation between markets generally higher than it has been historically; it also stays high in down markets. In 1987, for instance, when the U.S. market collapsed, non-U.S. markets also collapsed. Because the correlation is close to +1 in down markets, diversification fails precisely when investors need it most.

Summary. Although the correlation between U.S. and EAFE stocks is close to +1, I am nevertheless unconvinced that investors should give up on international diversification. As Figure 5 shows, the correlation has jumped around markedly during the 1988–2001 period, and I would not necessarily take the past few years as an indication of future market behavior (i.e., continued high or increasing correlations). In addition, company valuations are not the same throughout the world. In fact, some brokerage company research involving matched pairs of multinational companies, such as Motorola and Nokia Corporation, shows that the valuation of the non-U.S. company is often relatively more attractive than the valuation of the U.S. company. Although the markets tend to move together, an active manager might want to own the stock of Nokia rather than Motorola or TotalFinaElf rather than Exxon Mobil Corporation.

Currency fluctuations also affect the potential benefits of international diversification, although the traditional reason for investing X percent of a domestic portfolio in international stocks may have lost some luster temporarily because global equity markets are moving so closely together. As Solnik discusses, active managers should nevertheless continue to analyze securities in international markets relative to domestic markets to take advantage of valuation differences, to position portfolios to benefit from potential currency realignments (for instance, in the case of a likely weakening dollar), and to monitor the future correlation trends between U.S. and non-U.S. stocks to detect any trend reversals.

Good Diversifiers

Real estate—in the form of REITs (real estate investment trusts)—bonds, and TIPS are three asset classes that offer investors optimal diversification potential in the current market environment. These asset classes deserve a place in portfolios for the decade ahead.

Real Estate. Real estate investment is readily available to both individuals and institutions through REITs. Although REITs have been performing well for the past year or two, they are still reasonably valued. They sell for about 10 times their cash flow, which tends to be lower than many other securities in the market. They also pay dividends of 6–7 percent and are the only asset in the current market environment that offers a dividend yield. Although the situation is not as good as it was a year and a half ago when REITs were selling at a 20 percent discount from their underlying net property values, REITs are selling today at roughly equal to the value of the REITs' properties. REITs are also more attractive than they have been in the past because the office buildings they hold are "built to suit" rather than built as speculative investments; as a result, the overbuilding that was prevalent in the past no longer poses a substantial risk to the value of the REIT, and the supply and demand of properties seems to be well balanced.

Figure 6 illustrates the most important reason REITs deserve a place in investors' portfolios: The correlation between the S&P 500 and the National Association of Real Estate Investment Trusts (NAREIT) Equity Index has recently been close to zero. About 10 years ago, when REITs behaved like small-cap stocks, the correlation with the equity market was quite high—in the neighborhood of 0.9, which was long before such investors as Sam Zell, chairman of Equity Residential Properties and Equity Office Properties, purchased a number of the small REITs in the market. REITs today are a different breed from the REITs of the 1980s; they are now multibillion-dollar-cap stocks. Even if the correlation of the U.S. equity market and REITs does not remain at zero, it is not likely to return to a correlation as high as 0.8 or 0.9 because REITs have changed so dramatically. REITs are, therefore, one of the most attractively priced asset classes in the U.S. market and are good diversifiers. The data also suggest that the correlations between REITs and European stocks are low.

Bonds. High-quality long-term bonds currently are earning about a 7 percent annual return in the United States, whereas high-yield bonds of equal maturity are offering an annual return of around 12 percent. Although the realization of a 12 percent annual return is not often the case because of defaults, even with an average level of defaults, high-yield bonds offer high single-digit total returns. Bonds, therefore, can offer very attractive yields, particularly if one believes that equity markets are not likely to earn the 10.7 percent annual return that they have historically;[4] rather, investors will be lucky to achieve high single-digit returns from equities. According to Ibbotson data, stocks have historically returned, on average, roughly 5 percentage points more than bonds—otherwise known as the "equity risk premium." My belief, however, is that stocks and bonds are priced much more closely together now. Therefore, the equity risk premium cannot be expected to be as high as the 5–6 percentage points that has been experienced in the past.[5]

The correlation between the S&P 500 Index and the Lehman Brothers Government/Credit Bond Index shown in **Figure 7** illustrates that bonds and U.S. stocks have had a strong negative correlation since the late-1990s, which is exactly the diversification criterion investors look for in an asset class. From the present vantage point, the expected return of

Figure 6. Quarterly Rolling Four-Year Correlation between S&P 500 Index and NAREIT Equity Index, December 1983–September 2001

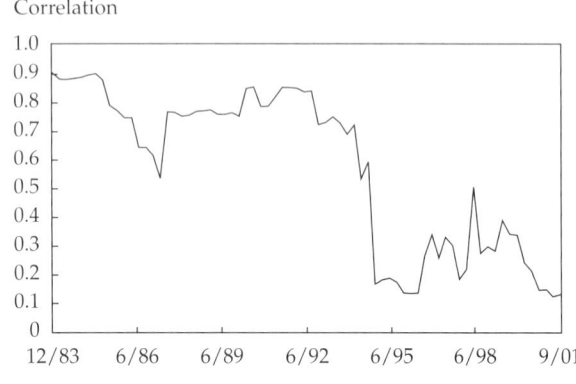

Note: Sixteen-quarter end dates.

Figure 7. Quarterly Rolling Four-Year Correlation between S&P 500 Index and Lehman Brothers Government/Credit Bond Index, December 1983–September 2001

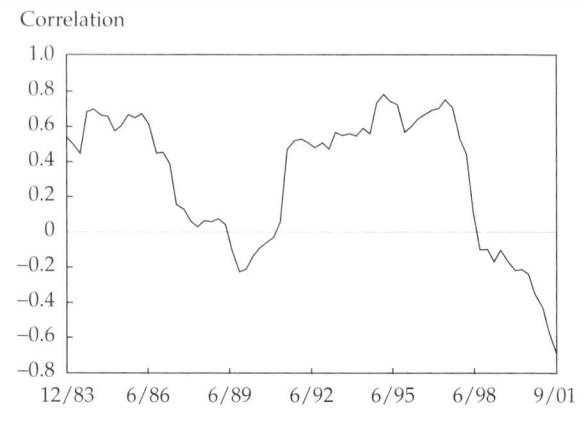

Note: Sixteen-quarter end dates.

[4] Based on data from Ibbotson Associates.
[5] For further discussion on the equity risk premium, go to the "Equity Risk Premium Forum" under Additional Publications at www.aimrpubs.org.

bonds is closer to the expected return of equities than at any time in recent history, which makes bonds especially attractive on a relative return basis.

TIPS. TIPS pay a base interest rate plus a spread that is indexed to the change in the U.S. Consumer Price Index (CPI). The 10-year TIPS maturity (as of mid-July 2002) yields around 3.25 percent plus the inflation rate, which has averaged about 2 percent for the past 12 months. Thus, TIPS currently provide a return of about 5.25 percent; if the inflation rate increases to, say, 4.75 percent, then TIPS will yield 8 percent, and if the inflation rate falls to 1 percent, then their return will fall to 4.25 percent.

Figure 8 shows the correlation between the S&P 500 and TIPS from March 1980 to September 2001. I calculated correlation coefficients extending back to the 1980s as follows. I began by estimating hypothetical TIPS returns for the 1980s and 1990s by adding the applicable inflation rate for those years to the 3.25 percent TIPS base rate. In fact, investors would have earned a very good rate of return from TIPS during the study period. The correlation between TIPS and the S&P 500 has fluctuated around zero but has primarily been negative for the entire 20-year period. TIPS are thus an excellent diversifier. TIPS also provide good diversification in markets when the S&P 500 is falling, unlike the positive correlation exhibited by EAFE with the S&P 500.

Figure 8. Quarterly Rolling Four-Year Correlation between S&P 500 Index and TIPS, December 1983–September 2001

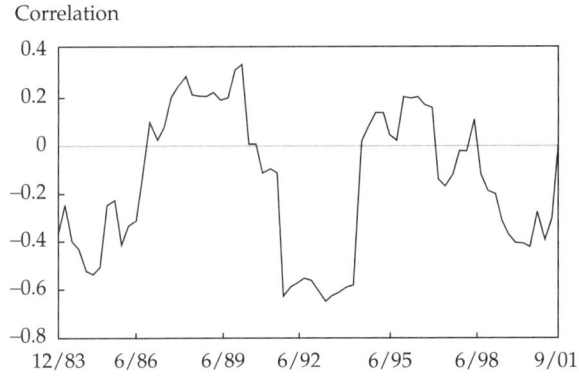

Note: Sixteen-quarter end dates.

Perhaps more important, TIPS are the only asset class that provide dependable protection from inflation risk. What if OPEC suddenly grows stronger, Europe starts recovering, Japan miraculously turns the corner, and inflation returns in full force? I am not saying those events will necessarily happen, but even with a modest increase in inflation, TIPS are the only asset class that will be of any benefit to investors. If inflation rises to 5 percent or 6 percent, neither common stocks nor non-TIPS bonds are likely to perform well. The possibilities of a worldwide recovery and inflationary pressure, therefore, make this asset class a top choice for a truly diversified portfolio.

Traditional versus Nontraditional Portfolio. A comparison of a traditional portfolio—composed of the S&P 500 Index, U.S. long-term government bonds (LT Gvt), and U.S. 30-day T-bills—and a nontraditional portfolio—composed of the traditional asset classes plus TIPS and the NAREIT Equity Index—illustrates how these other asset classes can improve portfolio performance.

In **Figure 9**, the solid line depicts the efficient frontier of the traditional portfolio. Incidentally, if I add EAFE stocks to the traditional portfolio, the frontier does not change. So, if the traditional portfolio were internationally diversified, the efficient frontier would be the same. The dotted line represents the efficient frontier of the nontraditional portfolio, which clearly shows a more favorable return per unit of risk for each point on the efficient frontier.

Table 1 provides the details of the nontraditional portfolio's performance and makeup versus the traditional portfolio. A low-risk portfolio is defined as having a standard deviation of 5 percent, a moderate risk portfolio as having a standard deviation of 10 percent, and a high-risk portfolio as having a standard deviation of 15 percent. For a traditional portfolio, an investor willing to accept high risk would have a portfolio composed of about 92 percent equities and 8 percent bonds, whereas a moderate-risk investor would have about 57 percent equities and 43 percent bonds. In contrast, the nontraditional portfolio for a high-risk investor is invested 88 percent in the S&P 500 and 12 percent in the NAREIT Equity Index fund and for a low-risk investor is invested 19 percent in the S&P 500, 13 percent in the NAREIT Equity Index fund, 27 percent in bonds, and 42 percent in TIPS. In other words, to move to the left of the efficient frontier in Figure 9, an investor finds that real estate and TIPS have a significant role to play in portfolio construction. These asset classes are excellent diversifiers for a portfolio, particularly for one in which the investor desires a minimum variance in returns.

Indexing

The evidence since the 1970s indeed overwhelmingly favors indexing over actively managed funds. **Table 2** shows that for the entire 10-year period from January 1992 to December 2001, the S&P 500

Figure 9. Efficient Frontiers of a Traditional and a Nontraditional Portfolio, March 1991–September 2001

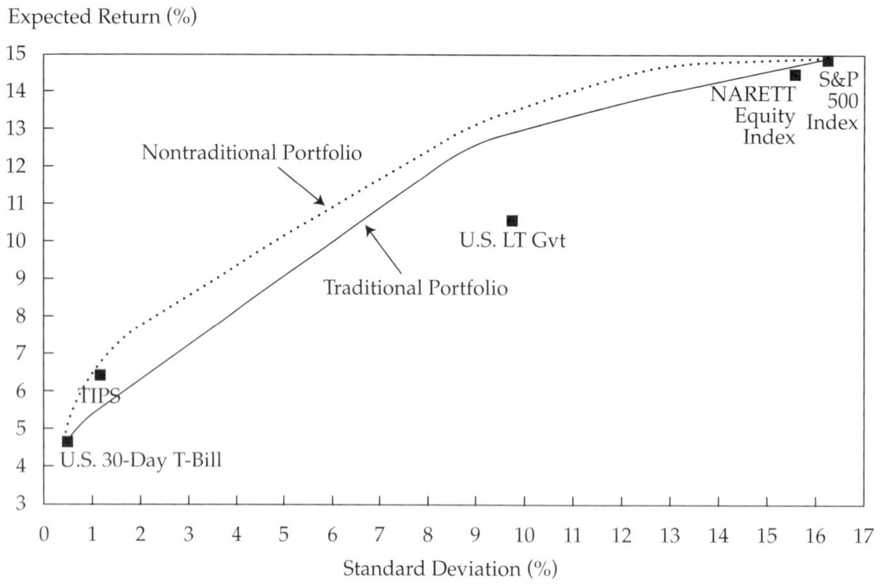

Table 1. Comparison of Traditional Portfolio and Nontraditional Portfolio, March 1991–September 2001

Characteristic	Low Risk	Moderate Risk	High Risk
Traditional			
Expected return (%)	9.13	12.98	14.51
Standard deviation (%)	5.00	10.00	15.00
Sharpe ratio	0.88	0.83	0.65
Efficient asset allocation			
S&P 500 Index (%)	22.80	56.54	92.34
U.S. long-term government bonds (%)	36.28	43.46	7.66
U.S. T-bills (%)	40.92	0.00	0.00
Nontraditional			
Expected return (%)	10.11	13.57	14.80
Standard deviation (%)	5.00	10.00	15.00
Sharpe ratio	1.08	0.89	0.67
Efficient asset allocation			
S&P 500 Index (%)	18.65	39.23	88.20
U.S. long-term government bonds (%)	26.74	26.93	0.00
U.S. T-bills (%)	0.00	0.00	0.00
TIPS (%)	41.53	0.00	0.00
NAREIT Equity Index (%)	13.08	33.85	11.80

Note: The average risk-free rate during the period was 4.71 percent.

outperformed 71 percent of the active managers of general equity funds in the United States. **Table 3** shows that the median total returns of large-cap equity mutual funds (which have higher expenses than index funds) lagged the S&P 500 by almost 200 bps over various periods ending December 2001. One might argue that in almost any given year in the past 10 years, 29 percent of equity funds beat the S&P 500, but no one knows in advance which funds will outperform the market. The best funds of the 1970s underperformed in the 1980s, and the best funds in the 1980s underperformed in the 1990s. Picking those funds that will beat the market is a challenge of mammoth proportions.

Table 2. Percentage of General Equity Funds Outperformed by the S&P 500 Index, Periods Ending in December 2001

Years	Percentage Outperformed
1	52%
5	63
10	71

Table 3. Median Total Returns of Large-Cap Equity Funds versus the S&P 500 Index, Periods Ending In December 2001

Years	Large-Cap Equity Funds	S&P 500 Index
10	10.98%	12.94%
15	11.95	13.74
20	13.42	15.24

Source: Lipper Analytical, Wilshire Associates, Standard & Poor's, and The Vanguard Group.

Table 4 shows that a similar situation exists in international equity portfolios. From January 1992 to December 2001 (the full 10 years), about two-thirds of active managers were outperformed by the European subindex of EAFE. Again, the problem is that the one-third that beat the index will not be the same one-third from one period to the next.

Table 5 illustrates that indexing had the same, if not more, positive results for bonds as it did for common stocks. Because bond managers' rates of return are far more compact, with the lower cost of indexing, a large institutional investor can achieve outperformance versus the market for a very minimal cost, only 1 or 2 bps. From January 1992 to December 2001 (the full 10 years), 90 percent of global bond managers were outperformed by the Salomon Brothers World Government Bond Index.

Conclusion

In the next decade, investors should consider the following aspects of portfolio construction because of past and expected changes in the global markets. First, investors should not expect much diversification benefit from international stocks because global market movements have been much more highly correlated over the past 10 years. Second, investors should consider asset classes other than equities for optimal diversification benefits. As the equity risk premium shrinks, REITs and TIPS in particular are currently priced to provide competitive rates of return versus stocks and are superb diversifiers because of their low correlations with equities. For low-risk investors, TIPS are especially enticing because it is the only asset class that provides inflation protection. And finally, even if the markets are not as efficient as I think they are, an indexing strategy should be a core component of every investor's portfolio.

Table 4. Percentage of European Funds Outperformed by MSCI Europe Index, Periods Ending in December 2001

Years	Percentage Outperformed
1	71%
5	59
10	69

Table 5. Percentage of Global Bond Funds Outperformed by the Salomon World Government Bond Index, Periods Ending in December 2001

Time Period	Percentage Outperformed
Starting year	
1996	57%
1997	80
1998	72
1999	93
2000	78
2001	60
Period duration	
5 Years	92
10 Years	90

Source: The Vanguard Group, based on a filter of more than 3,900 funds for portfolios with a beta of between 0.9 and 1.1 and an R^2 above 0.9 (final universe included 68 portfolios).

Question and Answer Session
Burton G. Malkiel

Question: Will idiosyncratic risk continue to rise?

Malkiel: I suspect that idiosyncratic risk will continue to increase, in part because of a change in the structure of the markets whereby news is disseminated almost instantaneously. In the past, institutions or security analysts received news before the average individual investor, but no longer. Now, with CNBC and the effect of people like the "money honey" Maria Bartiromo, institutional and individual investors tend to make changes at roughly the same time—when analysts first begin to like or dislike a stock.

For this reason, I am not a big fan of Regulation FD. I'm not sure it has made the market more efficient. When a company believes news is significant, then the news goes to everybody at the same time, and if that news is bad, the stock plummets by 30–40 percent. The fact that news probably is now disseminated earlier (through a "two-step" process) may have made the market fairer, but the downside is that it may also have made the market more volatile. In recent years, as compared with the early 1990s, certain structural changes may have caused an increase in individual stock volatility at the same time overall market volatility has been increasing. I think market volatility will probably decrease in the future, but individual stock volatility will remain high, which means investors need more diversification to eliminate idiosyncratic risk. Of course, some active managers want to take that kind of risk, perhaps to have more of an exposure to a particular industry, and that is fine.

Question: How do you reconcile the apparent incongruity of the volatility of returns in the market being trendless at a time when the idiosyncratic volatility has been increasing?

Malkiel: The article I wrote with John Campbell and others addresses this question. Individual stocks can be more volatile than the general market because the correlation between individual stocks has decreased. The volatility of the market is a function of the volatility of individual stocks and the intercorrelation of the stocks. My coauthors and I reconciled this seeming incongruity by looking at the volatility of S&P 500 stocks. In short, the volatility of each individual stock is higher but the correlations between stocks are lower, and the lower correlations have kept the volatility of the market from increasing.

Question: As Figure 2 shows, a 5-stock portfolio from the 1960s and a 50-stock portfolio from the 1990s have about the same volatility. How many stocks does an investor need to hold now to completely eliminate idiosyncratic risk?

Malkiel: You can never get rid of idiosyncratic risk completely, but to get to where idiosyncratic risk asymptotically touches the systematic risk line in Figure 2 (indicating the elimination of idiosyncratic risk) you need about 10 times as many stocks as before, or 200 stocks. If you want to get the returns of the asset class itself, of course, indexing would be the best strategy. Keep in mind, however, that idiosyncratic risk still exists when you index only to the S&P 500 because of the exclusion of small-cap stocks, which today are probably more reasonably valued than the rest of the market.

So, although 200 stocks now provide the diversification that 20 stocks used to provide 40 years ago, investors ought to index to the Wilshire 5000 through a total stock market index fund. Some investors have a core component of their assets in an S&P 500 index fund and then add an extended market fund indexed to the Wilshire 4500, but that is not the best way to diversify for the following reasons, as explained in an article of mine published in the *Journal of Portfolio Management*.[1] Indexing affects the price of stocks at least temporarily because when a stock enters the S&P 500, it jumps in price. A fund indexed to the S&P 500, therefore, incurs a lot of transaction costs from additions and deletions; similarly, when a company is delisted—for example, if Chrysler disappears from the index because Daimler purchases it—the stock's price decreases. And one should never index to the Russell 2000; 50 percent of the stocks in that index turned over in 2001. Investors should index to the total stock market to minimize transaction costs.

Question: What do you think of Professor Solnik's idea of managing risk by relating the number of stock decisions to industry or sector control?

Malkiel: I agree with Professor Solnik that active managers will probably want to choose stocks according to sectors. In other words, international versus domestic is not the issue. If a manager thinks the telecommunications sector, for example, which has a big bubble, has overadjusted, then that manager should look around the world for the best stocks to buy in that sector. I am skeptical that strategy will work,

---
[1] Burton G. Malkiel and Alexander Radisich, "The Growth of Index Funds and the Pricing of Equity Securities," *Journal of Portfolio Management* (Winter 2001):9–21.

but if a manager wants to pick stocks, then he or she should choose a sector and search globally for the best ways of taking advantage of that sector. And according to some pairs studies I have seen, some international stocks have a role to play in such a strategy. As an addendum, however, keep in mind how humbling this business can be. If I were to make any big bets, I would make them in the asset classes I talked about, not in industry sectors.

Question: What is your view on timberland investments and their correlations with other asset classes?

Malkiel: Before I answer, I would like to present my bias. I am a director of Prudential Insurance Company and chairman of its investment committee, and I work on the marketing of its timber fund. That said, timberland investments have low correlations with other asset classes, and considering potential inflationary pressures, I would pick timberland before gold if I wanted a real asset in my portfolio.

Question: Are there any asset classes in which indexing does not work?

Malkiel: Indexing to a small-cap index is unwise because transaction costs vitiate the advantages of indexing. The Russell 2000 Index, in particular, is very difficult to index to. I have also argued the same in the past about the EAFE Index. In January 1990, Japan was almost 70 percent of EAFE, far above the world share of Japanese GDP. The index strategy didn't make sense for two reasons. Not only was there a Japanese stock market bubble at the time, but an enormous amount of double counting in the capitalization of Japanese stocks was also occurring because of the way Japanese corporate ownership works. Company A owns 50 percent of Company B, Company B owns 50 percent of Company A, and because of the way EAFE was calculated there was double counting of market capitalization. MSCI has now corrected that problem by "float weighting" the index. When there is a control holding or a cross-holding, MSCI has tried to make the necessary corrective adjustments. Now, within EAFE, Japan probably has the right weight.

Indexing is also useful for emerging markets. Emerging markets are not as efficiently priced as developed markets, and these inefficiencies create a terrific advantage for indexers. Spreads between bid and ask prices are large, and trading costs are enormous, not to mention stamp taxes and so on. It is so difficult to trade in emerging markets that a more passive strategy makes a great deal of sense. And at least for mutual funds, I have found that the emerging market indexes seem to do extremely well relative to active managers.

Question: Because general equity funds include small-cap and micro-cap international stocks, isn't your comparison of the relative performance of general equity funds versus the S&P 500 an apples to oranges comparison?

Malkiel: The comparison I did was fair because I could have done it with large-cap equity funds and the results would have been the same. Of course, the results do depend on the period. And, in general, because small caps have not done well recently, I am penalizing small-cap managers in the most recent periods. But my 20-year data include many years when small caps performed better than large caps.

Question: Would you comment on the fact that the number of actively managed funds that outperform the S&P 500 has risen from 29 percent in the past 10 years to 37 percent in the past 5 years and to 48 percent in 2001?

Malkiel: In the past couple of years, the number of managers outperforming the S&P 500 has increased. Last year, Vanguard's S&P 500 Index Fund (after the 18 bp expense ratio, not the 12 bp ratio that individuals with $50,000 would pay, and certainly not with the very low expense ratio for the institutional shares) beat only 52 percent of active managers. That typically happens when the stock market falls, which is when index funds are at a disadvantage. Index funds are always 100 percent invested, but active managers hold between 5–10 percent in cash. Now, I don't believe that active managers are typically able to move from cash into stocks by flawlessly timing the market; for instance, the cash position of active managers was at a high the week after September 11. Nonetheless, active managers generally keep cash for redemptions, as do all mutual funds, including index funds. The Vanguard S&P 500 Index Fund, for example, holds 5 percent in cash, but it also holds S&P futures to make sure it is 100 percent invested, which is why the fund has not done as well in the bear market of the past couple of years. So, I don't think active managers are necessarily getting better; their recent performance is a function of the declining stock market.

Question: How do you explain the positive and often strong correlation between bonds and stocks over the long term, and do you think stocks and bonds will remain negatively correlated in the future?

Malkiel: The period when stocks and bonds both did poorly occurred precisely when inflation was accelerating. And if inflation accelerates, I would expect the correlation between stocks and bonds to increase; they would both tend to have poor returns. If that happens, however, TIPS will provide good returns. Inflation determines whether stocks and bonds will be positively or negatively correlated.

They have been negatively correlated recently during a period of almost no inflation. But if inflation accelerates, investors will have to turn to TIPS for shelter.

Question: If inflation increases, won't typical bond managers buy TIPS in their portfolios? Should TIPS be considered an asset class or a bond sector like non-U.S. or junk, and will managers hold them tactically rather than as an asset-class strategic weight?

Malkiel: Bond managers might hold them as an asset-class strategic weight, but I don't consider them to be just another kind of bond for the reasons I mentioned previously. I didn't discuss the correlation between TIPS and bonds and the correlation between periods of high inflation, but according to the analysis I have done, when inflation accelerates, TIPS have a negative correlation with bonds in general, whereas bonds and stocks are positively correlated. So, although TIPS are bonds, I think of them as a separate asset class. Whether an asset class is good or not depends on two things, its correlation and its expected return. TIPS could be priced in such a way that they would be less attractive, but where they are priced now, I think individuals and institutions ought to own them.

Question: Will the correlations change depending on the currency perspective between the U.S. market and EAFE, and given the flaws in index construction, such as the large-cap bias, can there be advantages in terms of diversification and investment opportunities outside the indexes?

Malkiel: EAFE is better constructed now than it has been in the past because some of the biases from the cross-holdings are out and the float weighting is better, but it still has a large-cap bias, which is a problem. I do think that there's a powerful reversion to the mean in markets; in other words, small-cap stocks outperform, then underperform, and then outperform. I never agreed with Eugene Fama that small caps are always going to outperform large caps. No one can predict the cycle of outperformance and underperformance. The valuations of small caps are better now, and I would hate to be indexed to a portfolio that was just large caps, and that's a fair criticism of the EAFE Index.

Question: Would you comment on the suggestion that the opportunities for stock-specific value added are much higher than, and may be superior to, the opportunities of value added through asset allocation?

Malkiel: I take issue with this suggestion for two reasons. Although a lot of idiosyncratic risk exists, an undiversified portfolio will have a much wider range of outcomes than it would have had in the past. In that sense, yes, there is more opportunity for differences in returns from holding an undiversified portfolio. Nonetheless, I don't think anyone has the expertise to be consistently right. A manager can be right for a while and can make good judgment calls, but inevitably, a period will arise in which that manager will be wrong. And if a manager thinks of U.S. stocks as an asset class and knows how to move between large cap and small cap and between growth and value, whatever those concepts mean, then that manager can outperform the market.

Nonetheless, having spent my career conducting research and listening to portfolio managers, I don't think people have the ability to outperform the market. Vanguard, for example, offers many actively managed funds that are controlled by portfolio managers who talk about their strategies and what they're doing. Once in a while, one of those managers has a good run. But my experience tells me that humility is the watchword. Even if someone thinks he can beat the market, he shouldn't bet all of his money on it because it is awfully hard to do and cannot be done consistently. That is why I recommend that people invest at least the core of their portfolios in passively managed funds. They can try enhanced indexing and make small bets, but I would not make big bets because of the idiosyncratic risk now prevalent in the market.

Global Considerations for Portfolio Construction

Bruno Solnik
Professor, Finance and Economics Department
HEC School of Management
Paris

> The benefits of international investing have been questioned recently because of the rising correlations between country markets, but correlations do not tell the whole story. In constructing portfolios, investors need to evaluate the rising importance of industry factors over country factors when selecting securities. And above all, investors need to consider company factors, such as where the company does business and how much business is done there, not just the location of the company's headquarters. Benefits from diversification can still be gained by investing nondomestically.

In this presentation, I would like to touch on three main topics: the importance of global factors on the pricing of equity securities, the implications of the importance of global factors for traditional nationalistic approaches to investment management, and the construction of portfolios to take advantage of global sector influences.

Importance of Global Factors

Thirty years ago, I was teaching at Stanford University and preaching for the cause of international investing. I lectured at a seminar at Stanford organized by Bill Sharpe where I asked a group of U.S. pension plans about their international investing practices. No one had a single dollar invested in foreign (i.e., non-U.S. and non-Canadian) assets.

Even 10 years ago, the investment paradigm was still fairly simple. Institutional portfolios had (and probably still have) a strong home bias. That home bias might be explained by emotional, psychological, practical, and physical reasons—such as lack of information and familiarity with foreign stocks and markets, higher transaction costs and management fees, and currency risk—but I think the importance of those factors is overstated.

Investors' approach to the international investing that was done 10 years ago was influenced primarily by two observations. The first observation was that country factors dominated the stock prices of companies and that the correlation of country factors was weak. So, the value of the stock price of Peugeot, a French car manufacturer, would rise or fall with that of other French companies, no matter whether the companies were selling luxury items or retail goods. The point was that the stock price of Peugeot did not move in sync with the stock price of Toyota or Ford or Honda. That observation was made by practitioners and was strongly backed by empirical evidence.

The second observation was the zero correlation between a country's equity market and currency market. When an investor bought Peugeot, the investor bought (at the time) a French franc asset. So, a U.S. investor buying Peugeot would lose money if the French franc fell because as the franc weakened, the stock price appreciation (in French francs) of Peugeot would not necessarily offset the currency depreciation. And in general, the country exposure matched the currency exposure, so the country allocation and currency allocation were the same. Ten years ago, the lack of correlation across equity markets made global country diversification very compelling.

Historical Asset Management Perspective. Clearly, 10 years ago, I could make a compelling case for international diversification because, basically, countries—France, the United Kingdom, and Japan, for example—and their equity markets truly differed. In terms of risk, the low correlations between equity markets meant that investors could reduce the total variance of their portfolios by spreading their investments over different countries. In terms of expected return, international investing was great because the investor could jump from one hot market to the next. If the Paris market was moving up, the investor could jump into Paris. And when it began to move lower, the investor could jump into another market, such as Japan. Through active management of country exposures the investor could generate very high returns because of the lack of country correlation.

The approach to global asset management was a two-step plan in which the manager first decided on a global asset allocation across countries or regions and then selected stocks and sectors within each country or region. So, the approach was based on a form of market segmentation. Think of a very simple fictional world with a French tribe and a British tribe. A chef from the French tribe prepares a magnificent fish dish with truffles and white burgundy sauce and a bit of spice, but its pricing within the tribe is very low because a lot of competition exists in the French tribe among restaurants. The British tribe does not have many cooks (i.e., not much competition), but one cook prepares overcooked fish and greasy chips that in a segmented world market are priced very high. Thus, in segmented markets, the manager searches only within the tribe for good investment opportunities. The manager does not compare opportunities across tribes.

In the segmented environment that existed prior to the European Monetary Union, an accounting framework was used in which every company was assigned 100 percent to one country, regardless of the location of its business operations. Under this framework, Peugeot was 100 percent French and Daimler-Chrysler was 100 percent German. Portfolio benchmarks were constructed with the same property (i.e., companies were assigned 100 percent to one country). Global asset management, or international asset management, 10 years ago was just essentially overweighting or underweighting countries. So, the basic idea was that each security was 100 percent allocated to one nationality.

Current Environment. The world has changed. Maybe 30, or even 10, years ago, that kind of international asset management was justified, but the international landscape has dramatically changed, and managers need to adapt. The main question managers are facing is whether the relative importance of various factors, such as country factors, has changed. If so, should they allocate less to foreign investment? And more fundamentally, how should the international investing approach be structured?

The financial markets themselves have been integrated worldwide for quite a long time. What is new, however, is that every single corporation is thinking globally. **Figure 1** shows the enormous growth in cross-border mergers and acquisitions (M&A) for the 1991–2000 period. As a percentage of global GDP, cross-border M&A went from about 0.5 percent in 1991 to about 4 percent at the end of 2000.

Figure 1. Cross-Border M&A

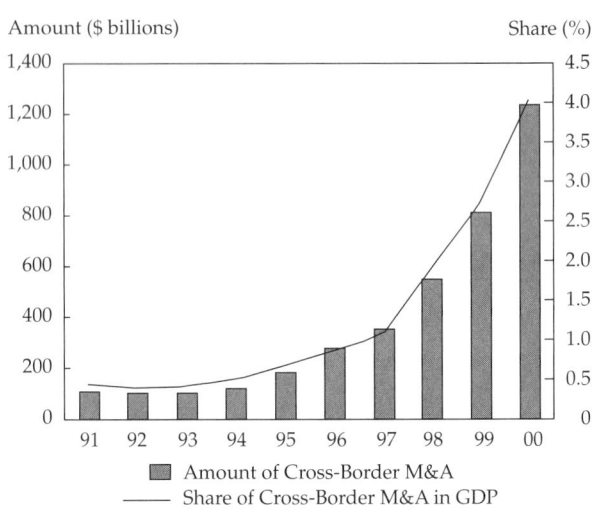

Table 1 shows that the capital stock of industries is becoming more global. Typically, 10 years ago, when a French company sought a growth strategy, it would buy another French company in a different industry and become a conglomerate. Now, when a French company wants to grow, it goes abroad and buys a company in the same industry in an attempt to secure a comparative advantage from its technical knowledge. So, as Table 1 illustrates, the percentage of similar product line (intra-industry) cross-border M&A has been rapidly growing, increasing from 50.9 percent in the 1989–93 period to 69.6 percent in the 1999–2001 period.

Thus, the really remarkable condition is that the companies investors are investing in have themselves become much more global. So, can country factors still exist in an integrated world where corporations compete globally? The answer is yes, but if a company is conducting extensive international activities, it should be valued, in an efficient market, as an international portfolio of activities. Take, for example, SmithKline Beecham before it merged with Glaxo. SmithKline Beecham is a pharmaceutical company and was one of the first mergers many, many years ago between a U.S. company and a U.K. company. Although it is headquartered in London

Table 1. Cross-Border M&A

Item	1989–1993	1994–1998	1999–2001[a]
Amount (billions)			
Similar product lines, intra-industry	$100.5	$488.7	$1,263.2
Across product lines, inter-industry	97.1	311.4	552.0
Total cross-border M&A	$197.6	$800.1	$1,815.2
Portion of total activity			
Similar product lines, intra-industry	50.9%	61.6%	69.6%
Across product lines, inter-industry	49.1	38.9	30.4
Total M&A	100.0%	100.0%	100.0%

[a]Data through 31 December 2001.

Source: Interactive Data Corp.

and has a very British character, it does less than 10 percent of its business in England. More than 50 percent of its business is in the United States, about 30 percent is in Europe, and the other 10 percent is in Asia. Investors should expect the stock price of SmithKline Beecham, in pound sterling, to be strongly affected by what happens in the U.S. economy because 50 percent of the company should logically be valued as a U.S. company; SmithKline Beecham earns half of its cash flow in U.S. dollars. So, all things being equal, if the same amount of U.S. dollar revenue is flowing into the company but pound sterling weakens, translating into higher cash inflows in pound sterling terms, investors should expect the stock price of SmithKline Beecham, as quoted in pound sterling, to rise.

Research Results. Quite a few empirical studies have addressed whether global pricing—company valuation—holds, including a study that I undertook with Jeff Diermeier in 2001.[1] The first problem we faced was how to define nationality. One possibility is using the location of a company's headquarters as its nationality, which is the traditional accounting definition. Another definition is the Barra approach, which uses statistical analysis to determine the sensitivity of the company's stock return to various national factors (e.g., an analysis of how SmithKline Beecham's stock price is influenced by U.S. dynamics). The third approach to defining nationality relies on fundamental business data. For example, using SmithKline Beecham's exposure to the different national markets in which it operates (50 percent in the United States, 30 percent in Europe, 10 percent in Asia, and 10 percent in the United Kingdom) to identify the factors that should influence the company's valuation. Diermeier and I wanted to determine whether the financial analyst approach to nationality matches the factor model statistical approach, because if it does, then investors have a useful tool.

To measure the exposure of a company's value to various factors, we used the following equation, or factor model:

$$R_f = \alpha_i + \beta_i I_{dom} + \sum_{reg} \gamma_{i,\,reg} I_{reg} + \sum_{reg} \delta_{i,\,reg} C_{reg} + \varepsilon_i,$$

where

I_{dom} = the return on the domestic index
I_{reg} = the returns on the regional indexes computed in their local currencies
C_{reg} = the returns on the regional currencies measured in the domestic currency

and the coefficients β_i, $\gamma_{i,\,reg}$, and $\delta_{i,\,reg}$ are the exposures to the various factors. The first factor represents the domestic equity factor; the second factor, or group of factors, represents nondomestic regional factors; and the third factor, or group of factors, represents the sensitivity to currency factors. I will not go into details, but our goal was to validate that the sensitivity we identified, the exposures we derived from a statistical analysis, were consistent with the commonsense results from the fundamental business data.

Table 2 shows the analysis for SmithKline Beecham. It indicates that the sensitivity of the stock price of SmithKline Beecham to the U.K. factor is 17 percent, although SmithKline Beecham's sales indicate an exposure of only 10 percent to the United Kingdom. The exposure to the U.S. stock market is 55 percent, which is consistent with the business data. So, even though SmithKline Beecham is treated as a U.K. company in any portfolio accounting system (in any benchmark), it is much more international and much more American than it is British. Thus, our analysis shows that the stock market pricing of SmithKline Beecham is global, in the sense that the geographical distribution of the activity of the corporation is reflected in the pricing of the stock.

---

[1]Jeff Diermeier and Bruno Solnik, "Global Pricing of Equity," *Financial Analysts Journal* (July/August 2001):37–47.

Table 2. Empirical Evidence: SmithKline Beecham, July 1989–January 1999

Domestic (β)	Foreign Market (γs)				Foreign Currency (δs)			
	Asia	Europe	United States	Total	Asia	Europe	United States	Total
0.17	0.08	0.31	0.55	0.94	0.08	0.11	0.27	0.46

Also note in Table 2 that the currency exposure effects on SmithKline Beecham are less than the stock market exposure effects. When the U.S. dollar strengthens, the repercussions for the stock price of SmithKline Beecham are positive, which Diermeier and I knew beforehand based on the derivation of the company's cash flows. But the currency exposures are roughly only half of the stock market exposures. So, if the U.S. stock market rises by 10 percent, SmithKline Beecham's stock price can be expected to rise by 5.5 percent. But if the U.S. dollar rises by 10 percent relative to pound sterling, this appreciation can be expected to have only a 2.7 percent effect on the stock price. Thus, we found that the currency exposure does not match the country market exposure, probably because of some form of currency hedging at the corporation level.

Diermeier and I found that investors are not stupid. They understand that the mere location of a company's headquarters is not a sufficient indicator of all the various influences on a company's stock price. Actually, strong evidence shows that companies are indeed priced globally. So, a company is really a portfolio of domestic and global activities. Furthermore, the more international the company, the more global its pricing. Thus, the percentage of international activity of the company dictates its exposure to the various regional factors.

One final point: Global industry factors are becoming increasingly important. **Figure 2** shows the relative importance, the ratio, of industry factors to country factors in explaining stock prices. In the early 1990s, this ratio was about 0.4. In other words, industry factors were much less important than country factors. The fact that Peugeot is a French company had a greater influence on its stock price than the fact that it is a car manufacturer. As can be seen, this relationship has changed dramatically in the past couple of years. Now, the important factor is that Peugeot is a car manufacturer. I would like to stress that this is a very recent phenomenon, which is very exciting. **Figure 3** also shows this recent change in factor influence.

Implications for Investment Management

This change in factor influence (from country to industry) has profound implications for nationalistic approaches to asset management. The traditional asset allocation approach, in which the manager overweights France and underweights Japan and then selects Japanese stocks or Japanese industries, is old and is no longer applicable. Defining nationality

Figure 2. Importance of Industry Factors Relative to Country Factors, December 1989–December 2001

Source: Based on data from S. Cavaglia, C. Brightman, and M. Aked, "The Increasing Importance of Industry Factors," *Financial Analysts Journal* (September/October 2000):41–54. Updated by UBS Global Asset Management.

Figure 3. Factor Correlations (MSCI Global Industry Classification Standard), December 1993–December 2001[a]

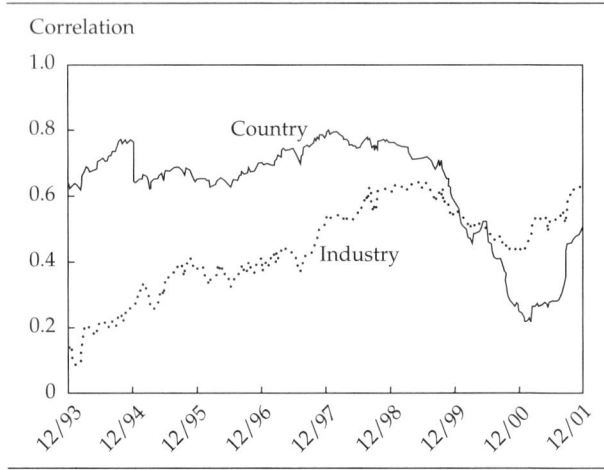

Source: UBS Global Asset Management
[a]Data through 28 December 2001.

based on the location of a company's headquarters and then setting global asset allocations is wrong. Managers should not use this approach. Although it is very simple and managers are comfortable with it, it does not apply any longer. The world is more complex than this approach suggests.

A direct implication of the realization that companies are increasingly global in nature is that by investing in domestic equities, investors *cannot* avoid global exposure. I will use Switzerland as an example. Switzerland is a very small country in size, but it has a fairly large stock market. If, as shown in **Table 3**, I do the same analysis for a well-diversified market-cap-weighted portfolio of Swiss stocks that I did for SmithKline Beecham, I find that this well-diversified portfolio has 60 percent international exposure and only 45 percent domestic exposure. So, even an investor in Switzerland who holds only Swiss stocks is holding an internationally diversified portfolio because the investor is holding many multinational companies. Note, however, that the currency exposure is very small (0.13) compared with the foreign market exposure (0.60).

When an investor buys stock in a Swiss company, the investor is buying a Swiss franc asset, but in general, that stock represents significant international exposure. So, institutional investors in Switzerland often claim that they do not need to buy foreign companies because of the international market exposure of Swiss domestic companies. But that position is very risky because a Swiss domestic portfolio is an undiversified portfolio. Quite a few industries are missing in Switzerland. And then for every single industry, the investor is effectively making an *a priori* judgment that the best company in that particular industry is by definition Swiss. So, if the investor subscribes to the view that a Swiss domestic portfolio can proxy for an international portfolio, the investor is tacitly assuming that, for example, the best airline in the world is Swiss Air, which maybe was true five years ago but experience indicates that was a very risky premise on which to base an investment process. Such a portfolio is full of idiosyncratic risk. This pure domestic investment approach is thus not optimal anywhere.

Today, the fashionable way to deal with the complexity of global asset management is to retain the country asset allocation approach while introducing a new asset class, "multinationals." The empirical research, however, does not reveal a special animal called a multinational. The more international the company, the more it is sensitive to international factors; it is a linear relationship. Big multinationals do not constitute a separate asset class.

And in terms of currency, investors need to be aware that companies are doing their own currency hedging in the course of their day-to-day operations. Investors used to have to worry about hedging only one currency—the currency in which the company's stock price was quoted. But now that conglomerates, such as LVMH, are hedging their own operational currency exposures, investors have to be especially careful about the ultimate effect of the currency hedges they put on in their portfolios.

The "balance sheet" approach to asset allocation is not feasible for global companies. The world is now too complex. The world used to be composed of many different tribes, and managers could simply overweight or underweight those tribes in constructing portfolios. But now, although individual tribes still have some importance, many other factors are at play. Today, for example, a cook in the British tribe may prepare magnificent cuisine and be prized very highly in the United Kingdom. But would that cook be prized as highly if he or she moved to Paris? Or to Chicago?

In this complex world, thorough analysis of a company is of paramount importance because a company's business typically cuts across borders and across other companies in its industry. To some extent the analysis should still be country specific, but it must also be industry specific. And above all, it must be company specific. Although this complexity brings with it challenges, it also provides opportunities for superior return and risk management for those with a good understanding of the global (and domestic) influences on stock pricing.

Constructing Portfolios

Constructing a portfolio to take advantage of global sector influences is tough. I am not going to give specific advice, but rather, I am going to discuss a way to approach the problem.

Table 3. Market-Cap-Weighted Portfolio of Swiss Stocks

Domestic (β)	Foreign Market (γs)				Foreign Currency (δs)			
	Asia	Europe	United States	Total	Asia	Europe	United States	Total
0.45	0.07	0.38	0.15	0.60	0.10	0.10	−0.07	0.13

A risk model used in portfolio construction should include two particular factors—country and industry. Country factors are still important and need to be taken into account in modeling risk even though they are secondary to industry factors. Clearly, global industry factors also exist and need to be incorporated in the risk model. If the portfolio manager can control for these risks, then perhaps the manager can take advantage of what I call "pairwise arbitrage." For example, TotalFinaElf is an integrated oil company. Its P/E is lower than Exxon's, so once the manager has controlled for all the obvious risks, the manager can compare those two companies. After looking at their cost structures, the manager may decide that TotalFinaElf is a much better oil company than Exxon given the companies' relative prices in the market today. Of course, managers still have to remember currency risk.

If managers can control for risk, significant alpha can be gained. The following simple example shows how complex the problem can be and how managers can address it. Suppose I build a portfolio that is long in Honda and short in Ford by the same amount and is also long in Lehman and short in Nomura by the same amount. What is the country exposure of this portfolio? Using the traditional approach of focusing on the location of the companies' headquarters, the net exposure in terms of country is zero. Because Honda and Ford are in car manufacturing and Lehman and Nomura are in financial services, the net global industry exposure is also zero. So, based on this approach, the portfolio has zero country exposure and zero industry exposure.

Nevertheless, two risks do exist in this portfolio. The first is whether the local industries are similar. That is, is the financial services industry in Japan equivalent to the financial services industry in the United States? The second risk arises from the geographical distribution of activity of the companies. Is Honda strictly a Japanese company and Ford strictly a U.S. company? Managers need a model that will allow them to control and understand the risks that they are taking as investors in this complex world. They must go well beyond the statistical tools and research tirelessly the companies they are buying in order to understand the risks in the portfolios they are constructing.

Foreign sales is one simple indicator of international exposure. **Table 4** shows the European sales as a proportion of total sales for the example portfolio of Ford, Honda, Nomura, and Lehman. If Europe experiences a downturn, the portfolio manager needs to know how the portfolio is exposed to the European factor. Table 4 shows that Ford generates 19 percent of its income in Europe, but Honda generates only 9 percent of sales in Europe. Nomura, surprisingly, earns 42 percent of its sales in Europe, so it is, in reality, a very European firm; Lehman, in contrast, is a very U.S.-oriented firm with only 7 percent of its sales coming from Europe. But because the portfolio is short in Ford (long in Honda) and short in Nomura (long in Lehman), it has a strong negative exposure to Europe.

Table 4. European Sales as a Portion of Total Sales

Company	Portion
Ford	19%
Honda	9
Nomura	42
Lehman	7

Thus, managers need to take foreign sales into account when assessing portfolio risks. Portfolio risks cannot be determined just from the location of the company's headquarters or the industry of the company; global and local industries can differ from each other, and the geographical distribution of a company's activities is not revealed by the location of the company's headquarters.

Portfolio managers need to move away from the simplified notion of constructing portfolios based on accounting measures and move toward the sophistication of what I call the "cross-industry, cross-country approach." The world is becoming much more integrated. The various tribes are interacting. A domestic U.S. equity investor is investing in corporations that do a significant amount of business abroad and that compete with foreign companies. U.S. analysts today should have the ability to analyze a company's competition, whether domestic or foreign. And the more integrated the global economy, the more important that asset managers have the capability of investing beyond the borders of their own country, even for a purely "domestic" portfolio.

Conclusion

Managers cannot focus only on domestic companies and ignore the rest of the world. The idea is to generate returns, and returns will involve companies that compete for business abroad and that meet competition from foreign companies even on their home turf. The world is changing in exciting ways, and opportunities exist for managers to make extra profits if they move faster than their competitors. Notably, financial analysis is becoming very important. If managers do not want to be fully indexed, they will have to spend more time analyzing companies.

A lot of people ask me what percentage of a portfolio should be invested internationally. I refuse to answer that question, because it is a silly question today. It is true that the correlations between all other markets and the United States have gone up. But does that mean investors should have less foreign assets, less foreign stocks, in their portfolios? I do not think so. Clearly, the approach is different now. The definition of a company's country (or location) is different from the definition used in the past, but if 40 percent of the investing world outside the United States is made up of Nokia and TotalFinaElf and LVMH and GlaxoSmithKline and so on, investors should consider those companies very carefully as alternatives to U.S. assets in the same industry. The very simplistic correlation-based argument of risk diversification is passé. Managers should integrate foreign assets into a more global analysis and deal with return and risk in a global setting. So, the question is not how much to invest internationally but, rather, how can investors afford not to be global in all aspects of their investment management approach today?

Question and Answer Session

Bruno Solnik

Question: Has globalization affected the correlation between international and domestic securities from the U.S. investor's perspective?

Solnik: There is good reason for the correlations between countries to increase slowly. As markets mature and develop, they become more integrated. So, the increase in correlations is a natural progression.

Nevertheless, a huge dispersion in performance still exists across the various developed markets. That is, the difference between the best performing and the worst performing markets is still very large for any time period that we might consider. But because the global markets have traversed a long bull market, followed by an extended bear market, the statistical findings show an increase in correlations. So, although we see an increase in correlations, statistical artifacts may be overstating the true increase in correlation. Investors should keep in mind, however, that other markets do exist.

Question: Are correlations higher because of benchmark construction problems?

Solnik: Whatever benchmark construction problems exist within a country become even more severe across countries. Sometimes the same company is included in two countries, and hence two indexes, so when the indexes are aggregated, the company is counted twice, which is a problem.

But I think we should not give these kinds of excuses too much importance. We tend to forget to look at the underlying fundamental values of companies and the determinants of those values.

Question: Is the growing importance of sectors caused by or related to the technology boom?

Solnik: It is not just the tech companies that are the common international factor. The trend affects all industries.

Question: Do you continue to observe that foreign-sourced earnings streams are valued at a lower multiple? Would you attribute this discrepancy to greater expectations of the risk of foreign earnings?

Solnik: As we all know, U.S. companies have a lot of foreign earnings. Apparently those foreign earnings are correctly valued because the stock prices of U.S. companies are very high. I would find it very strange if it did not work both ways. So, I am a strong believer in efficiency, although I think that there are some localized global pricing inefficiencies. I do not believe that the kind of wholesale inefficiency described in the question could exist. I do not think that foreign companies are mispriced compared with U.S. companies.

I do believe, however, that stock prices reflect investor expectations. It is clear that U.S. stock prices reflect the expectation that the United States is the greatest country from an economic efficiency viewpoint and from a regulatory viewpoint. Now, the question is, can the only way to generate high returns next year (because everything is already discounted in stock prices) be to have another good surprise—another good shock that expectations were even too low, that the United States is even better in terms of efficiency and productivity than was reflected in the current high U.S. stock prices? From that viewpoint, I might say there is a lot of risk in U.S. equity prices today because the information that is discounted in U.S. prices is already quite optimistic.

Question: Is the trend toward increased correlations irreversible?

Solnik: I don't know if anything in the world is irreversible. Historically, correlations haven't been stable. Some studies have shown that the greatest correlations occurring in free markets were observed in the period from the late 19th century until World War I. At that time, there were very strong correlations across a few developed nations, maybe five or six of the most developed nations. Then came WWI and the stock market crash of 1929, and the markets became uncorrelated. This sort of divergence could happen again.

Part of the benefit of international risk diversification is provided by new markets, such as Italy and Portugal, in addition to the traditional German, British, and French markets. So, I think the trend is increased correlations among the developed markets and more diversification opportunities popping up in less-developed markets.

Question: What is your expectation for value added for a currency management overlay?

Solnik: Currency is tough. Everyone has a different view. And currencies are very volatile. So, if the benchmark is really absolute return, and everyone has his or her own benchmark, you are sure to be wrong *ex post*, whatever happens. Even if you make money, you don't make enough. It is very painful to play the currency game because you always get punished one way or the other.

Yet, I don't see why currencies are any less predictable than interest rates. Furthermore, governments (and even supergovernments, such as the European Union) play the currency game, and we know historically that they tend to be losers because they do not have any hesitation about spending taxpayers' money. It is not a zero sum game.

I'm surprised that a lot of people say that forecasting exchange rates is impossible. I would expect that currency overlays could generate profit if they are done properly. I think the issue is even more important today with a large amount of global investment and when even domestic companies have a lot of currency exposure. So, a totally neutral view on currency is not viable. We must try to estimate the long-term currency risk premium and formulate forward-looking currency scenarios.

Question: How should asset management firms best set themselves up to take advantage of these global factors, these industry effects?

Solnik: Being somewhat of an outsider, I have followed the directions that quite a number of firms have taken in this area. It is a question of mixing culture, time zones, and so on. Yes, firms need to have global capabilities, which is expensive. Firms need teams from different countries, from different regions.

But we also know that clients are local. The way you serve a U.S. client is not the same way you serve a Japanese or a British client. The situation is a bit complex. The research needs to be truly global, but the client servicing needs to be local.

If multinational corporations, such as Coca-Cola and Ford, have been able to expand globally, then asset management firms should also be able to. And we are dealing with numbers, not widgets, so it should be easier for us. And the kinds of workers that we have to manage are all doing basically the same thing. It is not like we are manufacturing cars. So *ex ante*, it seems to be easier for asset management firms to expand globally than for other companies.

We must succeed. There is no other alternative. How could the asset management industry remain domestic while all other industries are going global? Nevertheless, it is very, very difficult indeed.

Growth and Value Investing: Understanding the Sources of Excess Returns

Thomas K. Philips
Chief Investment Officer
Paradigm Asset Management Company
New York City

> Growth and value investing in theory (as described in the academic literature) is quite different from growth and value investing in practice (as carried out by investors). A theory, the Fundamental Theorem of Growth Equality, is proposed that states that over time, the earnings growth of value and growth stocks is about the same. The index construction methodology of growth and value indexes (notably the periodic rebalancing to equal capitalizations in each index) is largely responsible for this equality in long-term growth rates, which has implications for the value premium, the size premium, and the importance of dividend equivalents in growth and value investing.

Value stocks over the long run, and I stress the long run, have higher returns than growth stocks. But as I will show in this presentation, a number of very subtle issues are associated with value investing. I will start by addressing the history of value investing. Then, I will discuss value investing in theory (the *Journal of Finance* version of value investing) and value investing in practice (what portfolio managers do for a living, which by and large means buying an active product that looks like an index or an actual index product). I will then go on to address EPS growth versus economic growth for growth and value investing, which will lead me to the Fundamental Theorem of Growth Equality. To illustrate this theorem, I will provide several examples. As I will show, the process of index construction has enormous implications for the nature and the source of value returns and has enormous implications for how return differentials between two or more indexes are realized. Finally, I will touch on the implications for the size premium and index construction methodologies.

Evolution of Value Investing

A very rough definition of value investing is the business of buying businesses for less than they are worth, an idea initially associated with Benjamin Graham. A crude expansion of that definition is that value investors tend to be balance sheet investors and growth investors tend to be income statement investors. That statement captures the essence of the two philosophies, but the lines are becoming increasingly blurred.

The notion of what constitutes value investing, what constitutes buying a business for less than it is worth, has clearly evolved over time. Benjamin Graham was perhaps the first person to use the term "value investing," and his notion of value was inextricably linked with buying companies for less than their net current assets. Executing a value strategy in Graham's eyes meant that investors would buy stocks that were selling for less than two-thirds of their net current assets and sell them as soon as they rose to roughly the value of their net current assets. Investors played this game for many years until the bull market of the 1960s and early 1970s caused these opportunities to disappear. Graham said at that time that the net current assets game seemed to be over but that value could be thought of in other ways, such as price to book. Of course, this finding echoes in the work of Fama and French 20 years later in the 1990s.

So, in what other ways can value can be defined? Sanjoy Basu showed in the late 1970s that low-P/E stocks performed better than high-P/E stocks. Thus, by making this observation, he captured the notion of value via P/E. In recent years, the accounting folks—Jim Ohlson, Gerald Feltham, Charles M.C.

Lee, Bhaskaran Swaminathan, and so on—have combined book to price (B/P) and earnings to price (E/P) into a single value measure, V. They have shown that the ratio of V to price is a terrific value variable.

The literature of value investing is so rich that the mention of these few studies cannot do it justice. But at an aggregate level, at an index level, all of these definitions of value are roughly similar.

Value Investing: Theory vs. Practice

In the academic—the typical *Journal of Finance*—approach to value, a value variable (B/P, P/E, cash flow to price, dividend yield, etc.) is used to sort and rank a universe of stocks (maybe the 1,000 biggest stocks in the world or the entire Compustat universe) from high to low. The deep value stocks would be at the top, and the growth stocks would be at the bottom. The returns of the top decile (value) and the bottom decile (growth) are then subtracted to get a value spread. The result is the value premium in the *Journal of Finance* sense.

But that is not the way value investors invest in practice. Typically, value investors invest through indexes that are all constructed somewhat differently, depending on the index provider. Each index provider takes a value variable (such as B/P, which is what Standard & Poor's uses to construct its indexes, or a mixture of B/P and earnings growth, which is what Russell uses to construct its indexes, or cash flow to price or whatever the variable might be) and sorts the universe of stocks using this value variable. The index provider then breaks the universe of stocks into two halves (two indexes) with equal market caps but an unequal number of names. One half includes the more value-oriented stocks, the value index, and the other half includes the more growth-oriented stocks, the growth index.

Periodically—every three months, six months, or a year—depending on the index provider, the value and growth indexes are rebalanced to equal market caps. This rebalancing is fundamental to many of the observed interrelationships in the value index versus growth index area. For example, the expected value premium is the difference between the expected returns of the value index and the growth index, and the realized value premium is the return of the value index minus the return of the growth index.

Several properties of these indexes bear exploration, and I will discuss them in this presentation. One issue involves the earnings growth of each index. If the S&P 500 Index is broken into a growth index and a value index (S&P/Barra 500 Growth Index and S&P/Barra 500 Value Index), in aggregate, their earnings growth rate must equal that of the S&P 500. But does the earnings growth of one grow faster than the others? Is one riskier than the other? Are the returns of one more volatile than the others? Are the earnings of one more volatile than the others? How do the expected returns of the two indexes compare? How does rebalancing affect all of these properties? And finally, how is the value premium—the difference in return between the growth and value indexes—realized over the long term by investors? Is it realized in the form of capital gains? In the form of dividends? Some combination of the two?

EPS Growth vs. Economic Growth

Before I delve into the properties of earnings, earnings growth, and EPS growth, I need to define "aggregate earnings" and "per share earnings." Aggregate earnings are the earnings that are associated with every company in the economy at any point in time. When I talk of earnings growth, I am talking about the growth of aggregate corporate earnings, which include the earnings generated by new companies that did not exist in the prior time period. The growth in aggregate earnings is the growth in the earnings of the existing economy and the new economy, otherwise known as "entrepreneurial capitalism."

When I refer to "per share earnings" or "EPS growth," however, I mean the growth in the earnings of a *unitized* portfolio—a portfolio that does not receive inflows of capital (e.g., an S&P 500 index fund). The growth of per share earnings can be no larger than the growth of aggregate earnings because per share earnings do not have the benefit of the influx of new cash flows. If an investor has a buy-and-hold strategy, that investor cannot realize the true earnings growth rate of the economy. The investor can only realize the portfolio's per share earnings growth rate, which cannot be higher than the aggregate earnings growth rate. That distinction is subtle, but it is important.

The rate of growth of aggregate earnings has to be the same as the rate of growth of nominal GDP. Why? In an open economy with a competitive labor market, the fraction of national income that accrues to capital, as opposed to labor, is roughly constant. Although it has varied between 4 percent and 8 percent over time, it is now about 6 percent and does not seem to be increasing. Therefore, the theory that a company's earnings can grow faster than the economy because of rapidly growing foreign subsidiaries, lower interest costs, and increased productivity is rubbish. The benefits associated with such growth typically accrue to employees, not to shareholders.

Shareholders tend to get a fixed slice of the national income pie. Warren Buffet wrote two articles on this topic that appeared in *Fortune* magazine, one in late 1999 and another in late 2001, both of which are well worth reading.[1]

And the growth of per share earnings must be the same over the long term as the growth of aggregate earnings. The reason is very simple. Suppose assets are always deployed efficiently in an economy. So, when a company earns more than it can reinvest in its own business, it pays out the excess earnings to investors in the form of dividends. Using those dividends, investors can finance new investment. And if the dividend yield—the free cash flow yield, to be more precise—is high enough, investors can finance all the new investment in the economy and can ensure that a unitized portfolio contains the entire economy. In other words, this assumption is equivalent to having existing firms finance all of the entrepreneurial activity in an economy.

This scenario does require certain elements, such as a bankruptcy court that redeploys in an effective manner the assets in businesses that go bust. But if these functions are efficiently executed, and by and large they are, then the growth of per share earnings will equal the growth of earnings. My claim has not been true historically, in part because the bankruptcy court has been erratic in its operations and in part because the capital inflows into most developing countries have been extremely large. Rob Arnott and Peter Bernstein show that over the long term in both the United States and the United Kingdom, per share earnings have grown roughly in line with GDP per capita, not GDP.[2] But in the future, I believe the growth rate of the two quantities will be similar.

The empirical evidence can help clarify my assertion. **Figure 1** shows nominal GDP growth as well as normalized S&P 500 earnings growth and EPS growth for the period December 1976 to December 2001. The earnings of the S&P 500 grew faster than the economy over this time period, which is not surprising. When the S&P 500 removes a company from the index, it is typically a small company in the throes of bankruptcy or one that has shrunk to a shadow of its former self. When the company is replaced in the index, it is replaced with a relatively large company. Therefore, it is not surprising that S&P 500 earnings grew faster than the economy. Per share earnings, in contrast, grew roughly in line with the economy except in 2001. This earnings implosion in 2001 should be ignored, however, because it was caused in large part by accounting issues and the true economic earnings of the S&P 500 in 2001 are as yet unknown. Thus, the evidence over this period shows that per share earnings grew roughly in line with nominal GDP.

---

[1] Carol Loomis and Warren Buffett, "Mr. Buffett on the Stock Market," *Fortune* (22 November 1999):212–220. Warren Buffet, "Warren Buffet on the Stock Market," *Fortune* (10 December 2001):80–94.

[2] Robert Arnott and Peter Bernstein, "What Risk Premium is 'Normal'?" *Financial Analysts Journal* (March/April 2002):64–85.

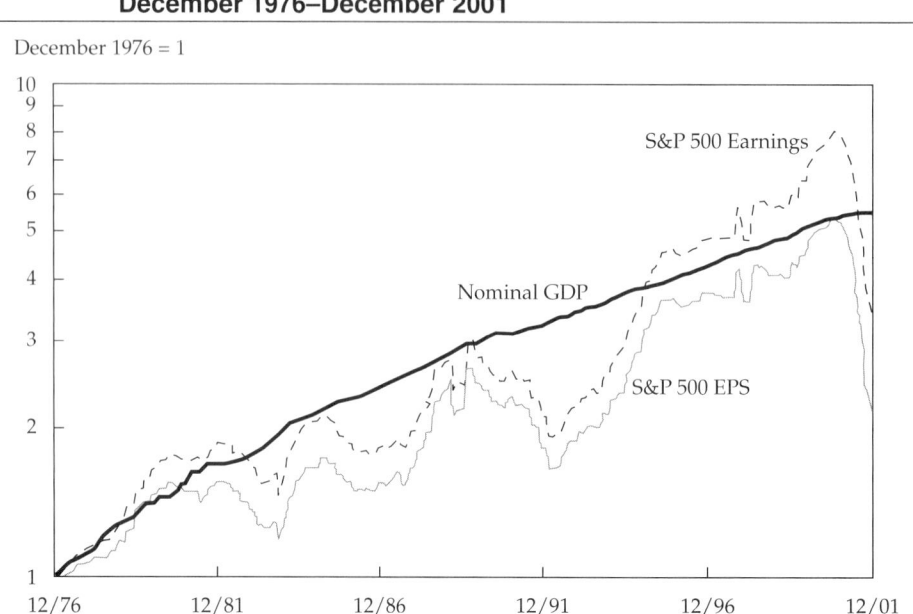

Figure 1. Normalized S&P 500 Earnings and EPS Growth and GDP Growth: December 1976–December 2001

Earlier, I posed several questions that I would like to address now: How do the earnings of the growth and value indexes relate to the earnings of the broad market? In particular, does the S&P 500 growth index experience faster earnings growth and the S&P 500 value index experience slower earnings growth than the market? Investors instinctively feel that S&P 500 value stocks have slower earnings growth than S&P 500 growth stocks, but as it turns out, the reality of the relationship is much more nebulous. I have constructed a time series of EPS and GDP data from 1974 to 2000—a mixture of data from Bloomberg (index values), Barra and Morgan Stanley's Quantitative Strategies Group (P/Es), and the Federal Reserve's FRED database (GDP). **Figure 2** shows once again the growth of nominal GDP, which is compared with the growth of per share earnings for the S&P 500 growth and value indexes. Notice that the EPS of both the growth and value indexes are not growing faster than the economy but roughly at the same speed. Thus, growth earnings and value earnings appear to grow at the same rate over the long term, although they have very different patterns of behavior. The earnings of the value index in particular are extremely volatile. In the 1991–92 recession, nominal per share earnings for the value index retreated to levels last seen in 1976. And in 2001, they again dropped to 1976 levels. So, value earnings implode in recessions and improve sharply in recoveries, but over the long run, they grow at about the same rate as the earnings of the growth index. Notice that the earnings of the growth index are surprisingly stable and track GDP quite well.

A good way to measure the difference between the growth and value growth rates is to do a *t*-test for the difference in means. **Table 1** shows data from three starting points and does not include 2001 because 2001 was such a horrid year for earnings that it cannot be used to draw any reasonable conclusions. The S&P growth index saw its earnings grow annually at an arithmetic average rate of 8.29 percent and a geometric rate of 7.75 percent from 1974 to 2000. The value index had growth of 9.25 percent (arithmetic)

Table 1. EPS Growth: S&P 500 Growth versus S&P 500 Value

Period/Index	Arithmetic	Geometric	Volatility	Standard Error
December 1974 to December 2000				
S&P growth	8.29%	7.75%	11.22%	
S&P value	9.25	6.45	25.26	
Difference	–0.96	1.31	20.82	4.08%
December 1975 to December 2000				
S&P growth	8.62	8.43	11.32	
S&P value	10.30	7.83	25.20	
Difference	–1.67	0.60	20.92	4.27%
December 1976 to December 2000				
S&P growth	7.75	7.60	10.67	
S&P value	9.84	7.28	25.63	
Difference	–2.09	0.32	21.27	4.43%

Figure 2. Normalized S&P 500 Value and Growth Index EPS Growth and GDP Growth, December 1976–December 2001

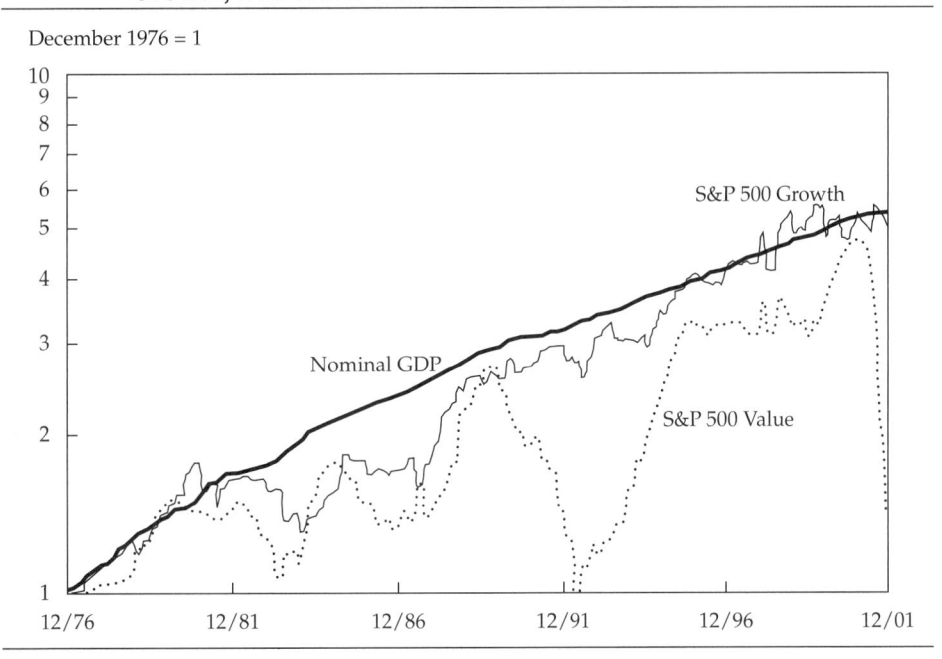

and 6.45 percent (geometric) for the same period. The difference between the growth and value indexes is about 1 percentage point (pp) expressed in both geometric and arithmetic terms. But how significant is 1 pp? The standard error of the difference is about 4 percent. So, the difference is one-fourth of a standard error away from zero (i.e., not really distinguishable from zero).

For the 1975–2000 period, the arithmetic difference in growth rates is 1.67 pps and the geometric difference is 0.60 pps; the standard error is still about 4 percent (or one-third of a standard error). And from 1976 when the recession was clearly over, with both the growth and value indexes starting from roughly the same base, the difference (geometric) in their earnings growth rate is 0.32 pps a year. The difference in growth rates is one-tenth or one-fifteenth of a standard error for the 1976–2000 period (i.e., completely indistinguishable from zero). Therefore, the empirical evidence supporting the equality of growth rates is very strong.

Fundamental Theorem of Growth Equality

Investors might reasonably wonder why the earnings growth of value and growth stocks is about the same. I have a theory that explains it, which is succinctly expressed as the Fundamental Theorem of Growth Equality:

> If all stocks have time-invariant growth rates, then all indexes that are rebalanced back to a fixed fraction of the market's capitalization, regardless of their construction methodology, must experience the same long-run rate of earnings and EPS growth as the market.

Following is an informal proof of this theorem.

Suppose I have a growth index and a value index. If the growth index has a faster earnings growth rate than the value index, then between rebalancings, I would expect the capital gains of the growth index to be higher than those of the value index, assuming no P/E bubble. But what happens when the index provider rebalances? Remember the index provider has to rebalance to equal market caps in each of the two indexes, so in the next rebalancing, a few growth companies will be kicked over into the value index. What happens to the value index? Its growth rate will be pushed up a little bit as a result. If the growth rate continues at the same fast pace, once again, at the next rebalancing some companies will be transferred into the value index, pushing up its growth rate even further. The net result is that after a while, the two growth rates will be perfectly equalized. Although huge discrepancies can exist for short periods of time, as I showed earlier, over the long term, the two rates must converge.

An immediate implication can be drawn from this theorem. If both indexes have the same long-run rate of earnings growth and if a P/E bubble does not occur, the capital gains component of return for these two indexes must be identical. Furthermore, any difference in return between the two indexes is entirely the result of a difference in their dividends or dividend equivalents. By "dividend equivalents" I mean all the possible uses of free cash flow: dividends, share buy backs, and takeovers.

Examples

Each of the following four examples reaches the same conclusion about the growth rate of earnings for growth and value stocks, but each starts with a different premise. I have called the examples "Only Cisco," the "Last Days of Disco," "Living with Risco," and the "Slow Death of Misco." **Table 2** lists information on the five companies used in the examples.

Cisco is a growth company with $100,000 a year in earnings, a growth rate of 10 percent a year, and a P/E of 100. It has 10,000 shares outstanding at a price of $1,000 each, which translates into an initial market cap of $10 million. Cisco grows at 10 percent every year; it never misses.

Disco, on the other hand, has $1 million in earnings, but those earnings will never grow in perpetuity. The company has a constant growth rate of zero and an initial market cap of $10 million.

Table 2. Company Information for Example Companies

Company	Earnings	g	P/E	Shares	Price	Growth Pattern
Cisco	$100,000	10%	100	10,000	$1,000	Constant 10%
Disco	$1,000,000	0	10	10,000	$1,000	Constant 0%
Risco	$500,000	10	20	10,000	$1,000	Alternating 0%, 21%
Misco	$1,000,000	–10	10	10,000	$1,000	Constant –10%
Mini C	$10,000	–10	100	1,000	$1,000	Constant –10%

Notes: Earnings are annual earnings; g = annual growth rate.

Risco is a risky growth stock. It has $500,000 in earnings and a P/E of 20. It too has an initial $10 million market cap, and although its long-term growth rate is 10 percent, the growth rate is not realized as a constant 10 percent every year. The growth rate alternates; for example, in some years the growth rate is zero, and in some years it is 21 percent, which averages out to 10 percent a year compounded.

Misco is a company that constantly misses its earnings forecast. It has $1 million in earnings today, but the earnings are declining at 10 percent a year. It has a P/E of 10 and also a $10 million market cap.

Mini C is a company that spun out of Cisco. Mini C is a small company with only $10,000 in earnings and a $1 million market cap. It has a growth rate of –10 percent, but it has a P/E of 100 because it has a new business model (as did most dot-coms during the bubble!).

In the examples, value is defined by a low P/E. So, Cisco is a growth stock, and Disco and Risco are value stocks. I will use the classic definition of value and growth indexes. That is, the indexes have equal market caps after rebalancing. In addition, I assume a stock can be partially allocated to each of the two indexes, which allows me to get around the granularity issue. Finally, indexes are rebalanced periodically.

Only Cisco. In this first example, the entire universe is only one stock, Cisco. Therefore, the growth index and the value index must each hold 5,000 shares of Cisco. This case is admittedly trivial. The growth index and the value index are identical, so naturally they have exactly the same long-run rate of earnings growth and EPS growth. Everything works out very nicely; there is perfect equilibrium, and no transfers are needed at rebalancing.

The Last Days of Disco. Disco is a company that has no earnings growth. It has an initial $10 million market cap, but its earnings never grow. Initially, the growth index is pure Cisco (10,000 shares of Cisco with a market cap of $10 million), and the value index is pure Disco (10,000 shares of Disco with a market cap of $10 million). But as time goes buy, Cisco's market cap keeps rising because its earnings are growing at 10 percent a year, while Disco's market cap stays the same.

Because the indexes are always rebalanced back to an equal market cap, a little bit of Cisco will begin to enter the value index. **Figure 3** shows the allocations to Cisco and Disco for the entire market. Initially, the market is half Cisco and half Disco. At infinity, the market is pure Cisco, no Disco. But between Time 0 and infinity it is a mixture of Cisco and Disco. **Figure 4** illustrates how the makeup of the growth and value indexes changes from Time 0 to Time 50. The fraction of Cisco in the value index is zero at Time 0 and rises to nearly 100 percent at Time 50. Similarly, the fraction of Disco in the value index is 100 percent at Time 0 and drops almost to zero at Time 50. By the same token, Cisco is always 100 percent of the growth index, and Disco is always 0 percent of the value index.

Figure 5 shows the per share earnings of these two indexes from Time 0 to Time 50. Notice that the growth index is always growing at a 10 percent annual rate. The growth index is always pure Cisco, whose earnings grow steadily at 10 percent a year. And because

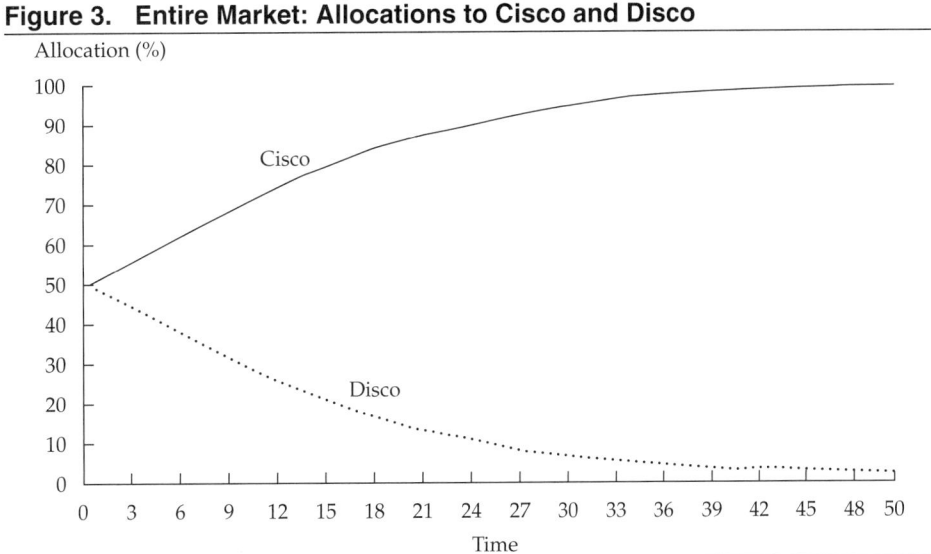

Figure 3. Entire Market: Allocations to Cisco and Disco

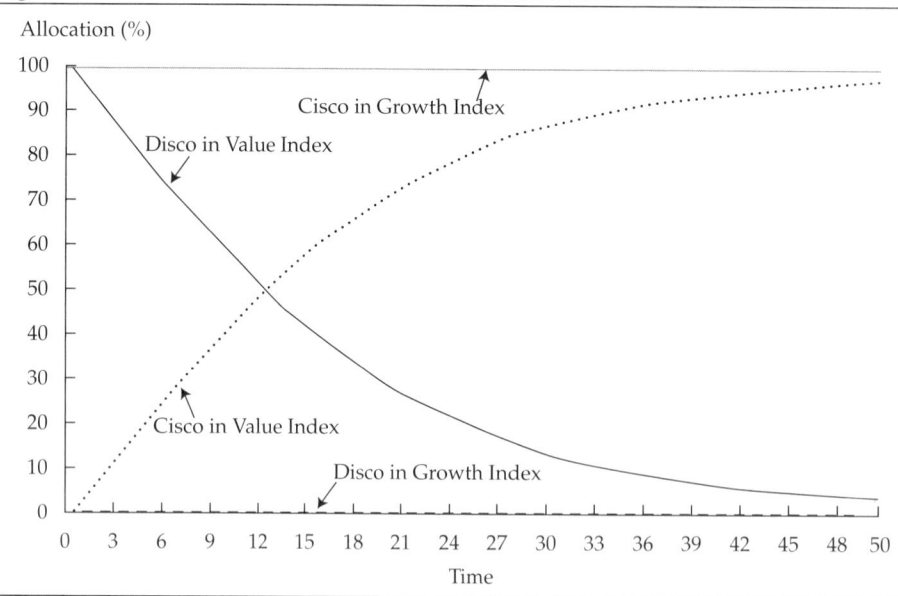

Figure 4. Value and Growth Indexes: Allocations to Cisco and Disco

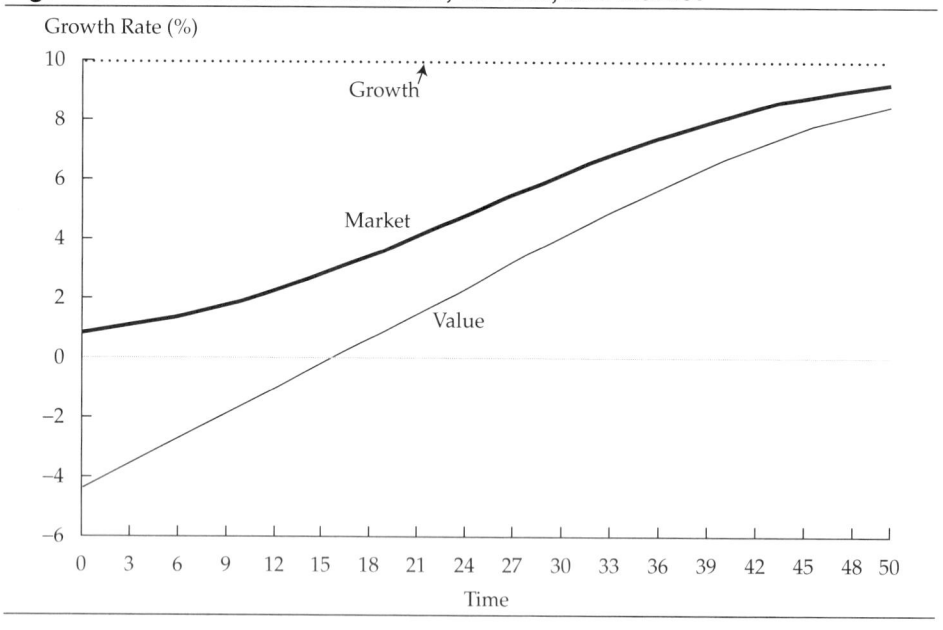

Figure 5. EPS Growth Rates: Value, Growth, and Market

the growth index never holds any Disco, its growth rate must also always be 10 percent a year. The value index, however, starts with a negative EPS growth rate, which then climbs almost to 10 percent a year.

The reason for the beginning negative growth rate for the value index, considering that Disco has a growth rate of zero (not a negative rate), is rather interesting. It turns out that the process of rebalancing has an impact on per share earnings growth. As some of the high-P/E Cisco is moved into the value index with the low-P/E Disco, the P/E of the value index increases. That increase in P/E is equivalent to depressing per share earnings growth. This point is very important: Rebalancing can affect EPS growth. To calculate the long-run rate of EPS growth, one would have to take the rate of EPS growth between rebalancings and multiply that number by the ratio of the P/Es before and after each rebalancing. That product gives the true rate of EPS growth for this rebalanced strategy. The fact that rebalancing reduces EPS growth by reducing P/E changes cannot be overemphasized. So, an index can have a negative EPS growth rate even though the smallest growth rate of any constituent stock is only zero.

In the end, the value index is pure Cisco, and it reduces to my first example, Only Cisco. So, yet again, I have growth and value indexes at the same long-run rate of EPS growth.

Living with Risco. The third example is much more realistic than the first two. The market is composed of three stocks, each with 10,000 shares outstanding—Cisco, Disco, and Risco. Initially, the growth index is all of the Cisco shares plus half the Risco shares, and the value index is all of the Disco shares plus half the Risco shares. As time progresses, Risco's earnings keep growing at 10 percent a year, albeit a noisy 10 percent—alternating between being flat one year and up 21 percent the next—while Disco's earnings remain flat. So, slowly but surely, Risco starts to displace Disco in the value index. As time approaches infinity, Disco's representation in the market becomes completely immaterial, and Cisco and Risco in equal amounts constitute all of the capital in the market. By Time 50, the growth index becomes almost pure Cisco, and the value index becomes almost pure Risco—although a little bit of Cisco pops in and out as Risco's growth rate alternates between 0 percent and 21 percent. And once again, rebalancing equalizes the long-term growth rate of the two indexes.

The EPS growth rates for the growth index, the value index, and the market are very volatile. They oscillate wildly around their long-term average. These enormous oscillations are the result of Disco exhibiting constant growth of zero, Cisco exhibiting constant 10 percent growth, and Risco exhibiting a growth rate alternating between zero and 21 percent. Because the growth index becomes pure Cisco toward Time 50, its EPS growth rate stabilizes. But Cisco's entering and exiting the value index has a huge distorting effect on the EPS growth rate of the value index, which is entirely caused by the change in the P/E of the index. Remember, Cisco has a P/E of 100; Risco has a P/E of 20. The long-term EPS growth rate for the value index is 10 percent, but in the short term, the growth rate is extremely noisy. This tendency for rebalancing to inject noise into the EPS growth rates of the value and growth indexes significantly complicates the proof that the long-term equalization in the subindex growth rates will hold regardless of the pattern of EPS growth rates experienced by the universe of stocks. If it were not for this noise, the proof would go cleanly.

The Slow Death of Misco. The last example illustrates the possibility of constructing a model in which the growth rate of one index is higher than that of the market. In this example, the market consists only of Misco, with a growth rate of –10 percent a year and a P/E of 10, and Cisco, with a constant growth rate of 10 percent a year. So, if the market contains only Cisco and Misco, the market exhibits zero growth. In addition, every year Cisco spins out an underperforming division called Mini C. Mini C has a –10 percent growth rate, but thanks to its new business model, Mini C has a P/E of 100.

From Time 0 to Time 100, the market allocations to each stock in the universe move from an initial equal proportion of Cisco and Misco to a final allocation of equal proportions of Cisco and Mini C. The value index, originally composed solely of Misco, ends with a 100 percent allocation to Mini C, and the growth index begins and ends the period with a 100 percent allocation to Cisco.

In this universe, the growth rate of earnings for the market and the subindexes is zero. And in terms of EPS growth, although the market shows zero growth, the growth index grows at 10 percent and the value index at –10 percent. Thus, in spite of the index rebalancing, the constant flow of poorly performing companies from the growth index to the value index creates a difference in their long-term EPS growth rates. So, in this example, the EPS growth rate of the growth index is greater than that of the value index and of the market over the long term.

Lessons. What these examples indicate is that the necessary and sufficient conditions for equal EPS growth may differ substantially and that the model of Cisco, Disco, and Risco is the right model for representing actual market behavior. Furthermore, because of P/E effects from rebalancing, short-term EPS growth patterns can be surprisingly volatile.

Formal Proof

The formal proof of this theorem is quite involved and can be found in "The Source of Value."[3] I will skip the proof here, but I want to point out that it contains a very important condition, the "no-pumping" condition, that ensures that the growth rates are equal. Remember, I said that the long-term EPS growth rate can be found by taking the rate of EPS growth between rebalancings and multiplying it by the ratio of the P/Es just before and just after each rebalancing. The product of the P/E ratios has to be bounded. It is equivalent to being able to constantly buy low and sell high, which should not be possible in an efficient market. Thus, the no-pumping condition is necessary because without it, someone will always be able to construct examples in which the EPS growth rate of one index is higher than that of the market.

---
[3]Thomas K. Philips, "The Source of Value," *Journal of Portfolio Management* (Summer 2002):36–44.

Counterexamples. That said, the results of the theorem are much more general than the proof allows and certainly hold true in practice. It is, nevertheless, tempting to construct counterexamples to definitely disprove the theorem, but I found that whenever I constructed a counterexample, I had made three or four classic mistakes.

The first mistake is constructing a strategy that is not investable—one that requires cash inflows at rebalancing. This mistake is not unexpected because confusing EPS growth and earnings growth is very easy.

The second mistake is neglecting to adjust for the impact of the P/E change at each rebalancing, resulting in either too high or too low a rate of EPS growth.

The third and most subtle (and the easiest) mistake to make is taking the view of a single investor: "I can buy this hot stock, and then I can move into the next hot stock, and then I can move into the third hot stock, no problem." An investor can do that for a while but not in perpetuity. The model has to address the market in the aggregate, not the portfolio of an individual investor that represents a very small fraction of the market.

The fourth mistake is allowing the model to create portfolios that grow faster than the market and that allow continual reinvestment without any limits.

Observations. First of all, rebalancing is critical to the argument. Without the phenomenon of rebalancing, the theorem would not hold. A big gap exists between the value investing found in the *Journal of Finance* and the value investing done by investors, and this gap is caused entirely by this rebalancing effect. Rebalancing equalizes EPS growth by transferring securities between indexes; the fastest growing subset becomes the market and is eventually distributed evenly between the two halves of the market.

Second, I did not use any particular definition of value in the formal proof. I did not predicate my comments on P/E or price to book or any other measure. So, the proof must hold for any definition, any pair of indexes, just as long as the market is split into equal parts. Therefore, it must hold for small-cap versus large-cap as well as for growth versus value.

Implications

Several implications arise from this theorem. First, if the EPS values of the two indexes grow at the same rate, then they must generate the same rate of capital gains over the long run, assuming no P/E bubble.

Second, because total return equals capital gains plus dividend equivalents (i.e., dividends, share buy backs, takeovers, etc.), if the capital gains components of two indexes are equal, then the only difference in their returns must come from the difference in their free cash flow yields. Therefore, dividends and dividend equivalents matter, and they matter much more than most people think they do.

Third, the value premium is in some sense a fundamental premium, because any split between two indexes must induce a difference in return based only on a difference in the free cash flow yields; the value premium is entirely caused by excess free cash flow in the value index. Following is a test of this implication. **Figure 6** shows the price component of return of the S&P 500 value index versus the S&P 500 growth index from 1974 to 2001. The capital gains components of the two are essentially identical. Although value stocks dominated the market in the 1980s, growth stocks dominated in the late 1990s, and the Internet bubble dominated in the period from 1999 to 2000, the annualized price return over the entire period is essentially identical. **Table 3** shows that the differences between the price returns of the growth and value indexes for each of the periods are within a small fraction of a standard error of zero. Thus, it is not too far fetched to see that the true mean is zero and the data simply show some minor noise around the mean. I use three starting dates to ensure that I have not simply picked a particularly favorable starting point to validate my theory.

Risk vs. Return. Two schools of thought dominate the explanation for the value premium. The efficient markets school says that value stocks are riskier than growth stocks and this added risk explains their higher return. The behavioral, or the inefficient markets, school says that investors exhibit biases in their investment decision making—in particular, they consistently overestimate the growth potential of growth stocks—and that these biases explain the higher return of value stocks.

The evidence that I have presented from 1974 to 2001 shows that the earnings of value stocks are much more volatile than the earnings of growth stocks and that the returns of value stocks are much less volatile than the returns of growth stocks. So, if an investor thinks that risk is measured by the risk of earnings, then the value premium is consistent with the risk-based explanation. If an investor thinks that risk is measured by the risk of return, then the value premium seems more consistent with the behavioral explanation. One possibility for the lack of clarity is that the time series I used is not long enough to reach a conclusion. Another possibility is that a "peso problem" exists. That is, for a lengthy period of time, value stocks can be largely unaffected by the vagaries of the market and then a particular catalyst causes the value market to fall apart, which is exactly what happened to value stocks during the depression. The peso

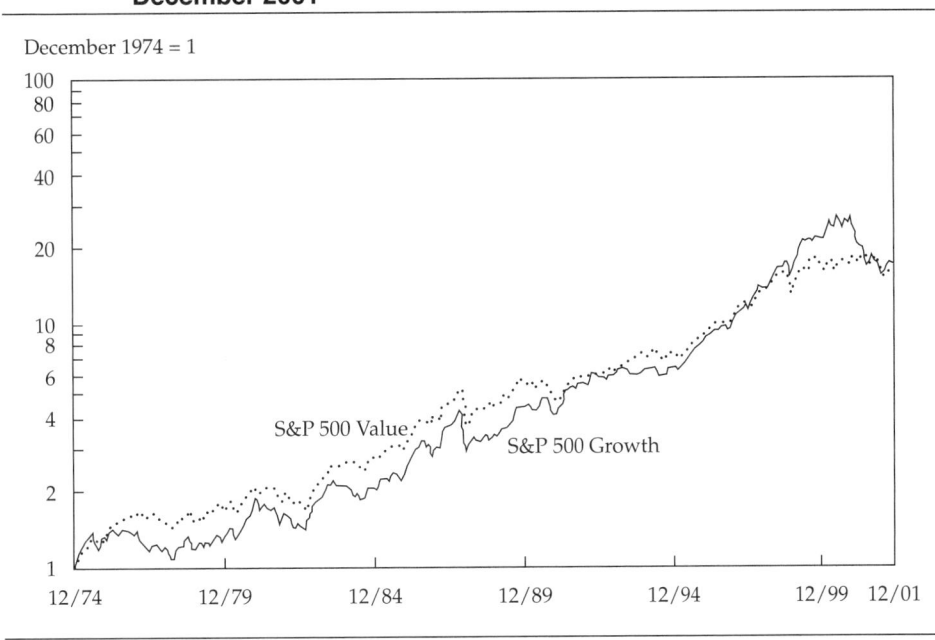

Figure 6. Price Returns: S&P 500 Growth and S&P 500 Value, December 1974–December 2001

Table 3. Price Returns: S&P 500 Growth versus S&P 500 Value

Period/Index	Arithmetic	Geometric	Volatility	Standard Error
December 1974 to December 2001				
S&P growth	12.53%	11.06%	18.24%	
S&P value	11.54	10.76	13.27	
Difference	0.99	0.31	12.03	2.31%
December 1975 to December 2001				
S&P growth	11.93	10.89	18.33	
S&P value	10.64	10.34	12.67	
Difference	1.29	0.55	12.03	2.41%
December 1976 to December 2001				
S&P growth	11.99	10.91	18.70	
S&P value	9.96	9.66	12.43	
Difference	2.04	1.25	11.65	2.38%

problem could be the explanation for the unobserved risk of value stocks. Therefore, my results are consistent with either view, and the question of what drives the returns of value stocks will elicit spirited debate for a long time to come.

Size Premium. I am very skeptical of the size premium. If my argument is correct that over the long term all indexes that are rebalanced back to a fixed fraction of the market's capitalization must have exactly the same rate of EPS growth, then the only way small-cap stocks can have a higher relative return is if they have a higher free cash flow yield. But think about two companies, a big company and a small company, in the same line of business. They have comparable fixed costs, so the free cash flow yield as a fraction of revenue must be smaller (not bigger) for the small company than for the big company.

I believe that the small-cap premium is a classic case of data mining, and a lot of evidence supports this claim. Peter Knez and Mark Ready in their notable *Journal of Finance* paper trim 1 percent of the outliers in the Compustat database and find that the small-cap premium disappears and a large-cap premium appears.[4] And Jeremy Siegel has said that by simply taking a few years (1975–1983) out of the study period, the small-cap premium disappears and a large-cap premium appears.[5] So, I believe that size is not a priced factor. The size premium will be sporadic; investors will see it every now and then, but it is not something that can be reliably priced.

Expected Premiums. Assuming the expected return of the market is about 8 percent, then the difference between the expected return of value stocks and growth stocks is about 25 bps, and the small-cap premium is actually negative. I expect that small stocks will underperform large stocks, although I am not particularly confident of this claim for a very simple reason: The small cap indexes (Russell 2000, S&P 600, and so on) are not defined in terms of a fixed fraction of market cap; they are defined in terms of the bottom 600 stocks, the bottom 2,000

---
[4]Peter Knez and Mark Ready, "On the Robustness of Size and Book-to-Market in Cross-Sectional Regressions," *Journal of Finance* (September 1997):1355–82.

[5]Jeremy Siegel, *Stocks for the Long Run* (New York: McGraw Hill, 1998).

stocks, and so on. Thus, more slack and more give exist in the earnings growth rates of small-cap stocks, but over the long run, I believe the per share earnings growth rates of small-cap and large-cap stocks will be equal.

Summary

All rebalanced indexes must have exactly the same rate of earnings growth. As a consequence, the capital gains components of their returns must be identical. Any difference in their returns over the long run must be explained 100 percent by their free cash flow yields (i.e., dividends and dividend equivalents). Thus, dividends and dividend equivalents are much more important than most people believe.

Finally, the size premium is in all likelihood the result of data mining. Furthermore, the expected value premium is about one quarter of a percent, and the expected return of the market as a whole is about 8 percent.

Question and Answer Session

Thomas K. Philips

Question: What are the implications for your theorem if the typical addition to the S&P 500 is a growth stock?

Philips: Additions have a huge impact, but it is not the impact that you would expect. Assume S&P adds a growth-oriented stock to the S&P 500 growth index. After a quarter or so, S&P rebalances the index. So, for a month or two, these stocks boost the growth index's earnings a little bit, but the effect is not long lasting.

The effect that most people do not expect to see is that because S&P is always adding big stocks, growth stocks, and high-P/E stocks to the S&P 500, it tends to depress the EPS growth rate of the S&P 500 itself. Figure 1 shows the earnings of the S&P 500 growing faster than the earnings of the economy, which results from the large-company stocks being added to the index. But the per share earnings of the index grew just about in line with the economy because of the P/E effect. Jeremy Siegel estimates that this P/E effect has caused EPS to be depressed by about 1–2 percent a year for the past 40–50 years. So, there is an important effect from adding growth stocks to the S&P 500; it is just not the effect that most people expect to see.

Question: You mentioned that the earnings growth rate of large-cap companies should be about the same as that of small-cap companies, but small companies seem to have faster earnings growth than large companies. How can that be?

Philips: You don't see the small companies that stumble. If GE has a hiccup, it makes the newspapers. But when a small company goes out of business, you don't see it. It might make the local newspaper, but it doesn't make the front page of the *New York Times*. A lot of those small companies go out of business, which cuts the earnings growth rate of the small-cap indexes. So, the weighted average of the two is about the same. It is the mystery of the missing observations.

Question: Which value benchmarks do you run your money against?

Philips: I think we could use any index without a problem. Over the very long term, it is a complete nonissue. Every index provider has something that sounds proprietary, but at the end of the day, the indexes are all about the same. In the short term, however, you have to make sure that your process reflects the biases of the index that you'll be measured against.

Question: You showed earnings for value stocks dropping much more than earnings for growth stocks in 2001. That doesn't make sense given the drop in technology earnings.

Philips: Keep in mind that I was showing index level data. So, for every Cisco that saw an implosion of earnings there was an Armstrong Holdings or JDS Uniphase that also saw an implosion of earnings. Much of the drop in earnings isn't real; it's just accounting write-offs. It is not economic earnings disappearing; it is accounting earnings disappearing.

Question: How often are the Barra growth and value indexes rebalanced?

Philips: Once every six months, in June and December. The Russell indexes are rebalanced once a year, at the end of June.

Question: Rob Arnott has said that the theoretical expected return of stocks is zero. How did you get an expected return of 8 percent?

Philips: Rob is not arguing that the expected return of stocks is zero; he is arguing that the expected risk premium is zero. A 5.5 pp difference exists in those two points of view. Rob and I discussed this issue at a TIAA-CREF/AIMR-sponsored equity risk premium forum.[1] My estimate of the equity risk premium is a little higher than Rob's but not hugely different. I would say there is a 1–2 percent risk premium, maybe 1.5 percent; he says it is about zero, maybe 0.5 percent.

But Rob also says that free cash flow is a very important component of return, and I agree completely with that statement because capital gains can only grow in line with the economy. Any excess return above those capital gains has to come from dividends or dividend equivalents.

Question: Do the value and growth indexes in your analysis exhibit survival bias?

Philips: There is a peculiar form of bias in the data, but it is not biased in that sense. The caveat is that the data are all backfilled. S&P created its indexes in the 1990s and, with Barra's help, used the Compustat tapes to value all the stocks that existed at any point in time. So, S&P was able to determine what the S&P 500 looked like at any point in time. Then, using that live data, it split the S&P 500 into two halves based on price-to-book ratios or the particular measure the Compustat tapes allowed it to calculate. So, the indexes are affected by the backfilling effect, but it is not a bias. The numbers are real.

---
[1] To view the presentations made at the Equity Risk Premium Forum, go to the Additional Publications section at www.aimrpubs.org.

Reintegrating the Equity Portfolio

Richard M. Ennis, CFA
Principal
Ennis Knupp + Associates
Chicago

> The current convention in U.S. equity portfolio construction of adhering to a multiple-specialist model tends to serve managers much better than clients. Despite some of the advantages of specialization that the model provides, increasing the allocation to passive management and using a "whole-stock" approach rather than multiple specialists both reduces costs and increases value-added opportunities.

According to portfolio theory, the risk of the total portfolio is all that matters. Institutional investors, however, typically divide their portfolios into smaller, more manageable portfolios for a variety of reasons. Such a multiple-specialist approach facilitates a broad selection of managers and products and enhances the opportunities for risk control and flexibility in managing portfolios. Nonetheless, conventional acceptance of this practice ignores several disadvantages, the largest of which is the failure to produce positive net value added. Big pension funds and other diversified institutional investors should, therefore, adopt a whole-stock portfolio approach using more indexing and fewer managers, although ones with broader mandates.

Traditional Portfolio Management Structure

Figure 1 illustrates a typical contemporary portfolio management structure for an institutional investor. In the interest of efficiency and manageability, portfolios are usually broken down into several parts, each of which merits its own separate management. At Ennis Knupp + Associates, we work with five asset classes, or subportfolio components. A bond portfolio, for example, is sufficiently different from a private equity or U.S. equity portfolio to manage it as a separate activity. Although each component has to be considered in the context of the investor's total portfolio, dividing a portfolio into separate components makes it operationally more tractable.

Throughout this presentation I will focus on one asset class—U.S. equity. As Figure 1 shows, the convention is to divide U.S. equity into passive and active components. The 200 largest defined-benefit pension funds in the United States typically divide the U.S. equity allocation so that 50 percent is invested in passive funds and 50 percent is invested in active funds. The active portfolio, in turn, tends to be divided among several specialist managers. The data for the same 200 defined-benefit funds indicate that they employ, on average, nine active domestic equity managers. Many use some type of completeness feature, whether a dynamic completeness fund or a sector index fund, to fill any style gaps. For multiple-specialist portfolios that use a completeness feature, the R^2 is typically about 99 percent.

Cost. Table 1 illustrates that the annual operating expenses for a multiple-specialist portfolio are approximately 120 bps. Management fees, underlying manager transaction costs, manager turnover (the cost of changing managers), and the overhead for selecting managers and administering the program all have an associated cost. For this strategy to break even, it must realize gains of at least 120 bps and must realize even larger gains if the strategy is to be beneficial to the investor.

Performance. Figure 2 depicts the performance payoff for the standard multiple-specialist model. The cumulative value added over the 10-year period from 1991 to 2000 of Cost Effectiveness Measurement's 130 or so participating large U.S. pension funds was calculated by comparing the performance of each external active manager with the fund's composite benchmark for that manager. Even though the cumulative value added shown is net of any costs,

Figure 1. Typical Contemporary Portfolio Management Structure

```
                        Total Portfolio
    ┌──────────┬──────────┬──────────┬──────────┐
Private Equity  U.S. Equity  Non-U.S.  Real Estate  Fixed Income
                             Equity
                ┌────┴────┐
             Passive    Active
   ┌──────────┬──────────┬──────────┬──────────┬──────────┐
Specialist A  Specialist B  Specialist C  Specialist D  Specialist E  Specialist F  Completeness Fund
```

Table 1. Cost of Operating a Multiple-Specialist Portfolio

Cost Component	Annual Cost as a Percentage of Assets
Management fees	0.50%
Manager transaction costs	0.50
Manager turnover	0.15
Manager selection and supervision, custody	0.05
Total	1.20%

Source: Based on data from Greenwich Associates, Ennis Knupp + Associates, and Donald B. Keim and Ananth Madhavan, "The Cost of Institutional Equity Trades," *Financial Analysts Journal* (July/August 1998):50–63.

the payoff has nevertheless been negative since the late 1990s. Active management, at least for this particular system of multiple managers, has not paid off recently.

An alternative test of the multiple-specialist model's performance would examine all available commercial multiple-equity-manager funds. Such funds are sponsored by consulting organizations and other firms or industry co-op types of organizations. These multiple-equity-manager funds select a group of managers to provide a package solution of equity management for clients. The efficacy of the multiple-specialist model could be tested by analyzing the data on most or all of these types of enterprises and examining their returns, net of fees.

At EnnisKnupp, we performed such an analysis. We identified 13 multiple-specialist funds that are managed by well-known organizations. As a hedge against survivorship bias and proliferation, we chose only funds that had been in business for five years. As **Table 2** shows, the 13 funds had, on average, a 12-year record, although the number of full years since inception ranged from as few as 5 years to as many as 28 years. For each of the funds, the net value added is relative to the benchmark that the fund represents as its benchmark. The funds were either large-cap or all-cap funds; no small-cap funds were included in our analysis. So, using a large-cap benchmark, such as a Russell 3000 Index or Russell 1000 Index, the 13 funds produced a negative return of 134 bps, which is approximately the operating margin for funds of this type.

Critical Appraisal

One commercial, well-known, well-produced, and respected database of equity managers uses 76 classifications to categorize active domestic equity managers by style. The periodic table of elements requires only about 110 entries, but 76 buckets seem to be necessary to properly accomplish the taxonomy of active equity management in the United States alone. As the number of specialties increases, the breadth of

Figure 2. Payoff for 10 Years of Active Management for Large U.S. Pension Funds, 1991–2000

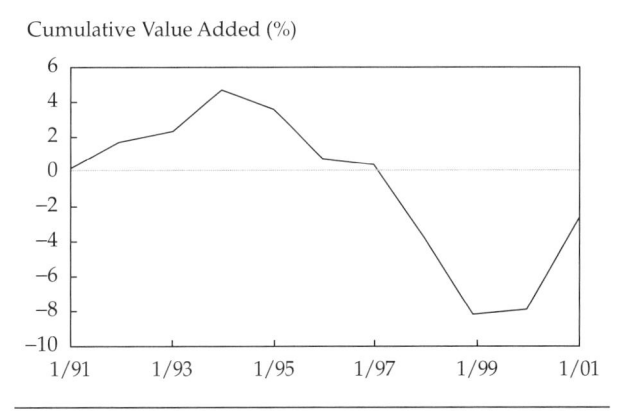

Source: Cost Effectiveness Measurement.

Table 2. Performance of Professionally Managed Funds of Managers

Fund	Number of Full Years since Inception	Net Value Added since Inception
1	5	0.72%
2	19	0.51
3	15	0.21
4	8	–0.50
5	28	–0.90
6	12	–1.16
7	11	–1.57
8	11	–1.82
9	7	–2.10
10	5	–2.30
11	12	–2.76
12	15	–2.80
13	12	–2.95
Average	12	–1.34%

Source: Fund sponsors, Morningstar.

each has to narrow. Yet more than 90 percent of the variation in return among securities is factor driven, not security-specific driven.[1] Therefore, by focusing on a relatively narrow list of stocks in one country, active managers are missing a lot of the equity market action.

Neither clients nor consultants are qualified to make strategic outlook-based judgments to move money from one sector of the market to another sector or from one stock to another stock. Such decisions are simply not within their area of expertise, which leaves consultants and clients in the dubious position of constructing a mosaic of money managers, similar to trying to assemble a jigsaw puzzle of various managers with different styles. Because neither clients nor consultants are qualified to make strategic or active types of decisions, they have to put managers in certain style "boxes." They have to impose a discipline on the managers to behave in a tidy manner in order to control the process.

In my opinion, the standard model has not worked very well. Although manager style characterization has made great advances in the past 5–10 years, the techniques for defining style categories are imperfect. These less-than-perfect characterizations of manager styles have created performance measurement problems for managers and have contributed significantly to so-called misfit risk. During the technology boom, for instance, stocks quickly went from being new issues to large-cap growth stocks.

[1] Eugene F. Fama and Kenneth R. French, "Common Risk Factors in the Returns on Stocks and Bonds," *Journal of Financial Economics* (February 1993):3–56.

The large-cap growth sector, which traditionally included only a negligible number of technology stocks, was suddenly dominated by them. So, for plan sponsors who were trying to keep all of their players distributed around the playing field in an optimal fashion, the situation proved to be a challenge, to say the least.

My critical appraisal of the standard model is as follows: It is very high in cost, involves great complexity, and produces an overall portfolio that has within it rigid and arbitrary boundaries dividing areas of investment style. Another factor that should not be underestimated or misappreciated is the burden that these shortcomings put on the client to be skillful, savvy, and astute. The client has to cultivate not only the ability to identify skillful managers but also the capacity to combine their skills in a portfolio without leaving gaps or creating redundancies. In other words, the standard model requires such a tremendous amount of skill on the part of the client that the client cannot simply be the client. The client becomes a principal actor in the process of active portfolio construction. Finally, the performance of portfolios using this structure resembles the cost of operation, which makes closet indexing, an issue I will discuss later, an apt characterization.

Whole-Stock Portfolios

I now want to develop the idea of a whole-stock portfolio. A "whole portfolio" includes all of the active management opportunities represented by an asset class. Although few parameters exist to define the term, I have identified three distinguishing characteristics, regardless of whether the portfolio in question is a stock, bond, or global equity portfolio. One characteristic is generality, which is closely related to the concept of breadth. As Ronald Kahn discussed, breadth indicates a wide and encompassing, rather than narrow, opportunity set.[2] The second characteristic is freedom—freedom for managers who have skill to find value wherever it may lie. The third characteristic is the idea of completeness; that is, the client can acquire a complete portfolio, or at least a complete subportfolio, and does not have to put together several independently managed active portfolios in order to try to add value at a particular asset-class level.

Types of Whole Portfolios. Simply put, the grid used by multiple-equity-manager portfolios for about the past 20 years includes value, core, and growth categories with small-cap, mid-cap, and large-cap subsets for each category; one, two, or three

[2] See Mr. Kahn's presentation in this proceedings.

managers in each category are then asked to focus on the best opportunities in their habitat. These rather arbitrary boundaries within the portfolio should be eliminated, however, so that investment managers have the ability to select from the entire opportunity set without any restrictions. Several real-world examples of whole-stock portfolios follow.

■ *Traditional.* An organization that uses a traditional approach typically has 30 or more securities analysts, economists, market analysts, portfolio managers, and quantitative analysts conducting fundamental research and trying to identify mispriced securities. They then select the securities and combine them in a portfolio to achieve the highest possible information ratio.

■ *Quantitative.* A quantitative approach is similar to a traditional approach in its attempt to identify security mispricings and efficiently translate those mispricings into a portfolio that maximizes the information ratio. It is a less intuitive and more disciplined process in some respects, however, and is subject to very direct and explicit forms of risk control.

■ *Combined specialties.* Some firms offer a whole-portfolio capability by making themselves the master portfolio manager. These days, it is not uncommon for an equity manager to have products in most, if not all, of the style categories, including REITs (real estate investment trusts) and special situations. Firms have created these various capabilities and have large-cap products and value and growth orientations. And some firms offer to combine their specialty portfolios and will fashion for clients a whole portfolio so that the clients do not have to be in the business of attempting to do it themselves.

■ *Long–short market neutral.* In some respects, a long–short market-neutral portfolio, as long as it is being applied across a sufficiently broad opportunity set, may be the ultimate whole-stock portfolio, at least to the extent that the long-only constraint really is a constraint and operates to lessen breadth in the portfolio. A long–short market-neutral strategy has the potential for offering substantial breadth as well as freedom.

■ *Hybrid.* Many firms take multiple approaches. They employ traditional analysts, use quantitative methods, and apply more than one developed product but nevertheless share certain features that embrace the generality and complexity of the stock market. They also give the manager a degree of freedom that the current structure does not. And last but not least, in all cases, the manager, not the client, is responsible for portfolio construction.

Precedent for Whole Portfolios. I will now examine how the practice of managing U.S. equity portfolios has evolved in comparison with closely related types of portfolios, namely, fixed income and international equity.

■ *Fixed income.* Unlike in U.S. equities, in fixed income, both buyers and sellers have largely avoided the fragmentation of portfolios, mostly thanks to the core-plus concept. Leading fixed-income managers invest not only in U.S. Treasuries and investment-grade corporate bonds but also in mortgage securities, with their complex optionality, and junk bonds, with all the labor-intensive and complex credit work required to maintain active investments in below-investment-grade bonds. Fixed-income managers also invest in emerging market and nondollar debt, which requires the ability to effectively manage foreign exchange exposure.

In fixed income, managers have opted to engage the complexity of the fixed-income market, which constantly reinvents itself with the cycle of maturing issues and new issues and, therefore, represents a new challenge every day in terms of its complexity and breadth. For the most part, clients have elected to avail themselves of this approach. Some of our large state pension fund clients create specialist bond portfolio managers, but as a practical matter, the mainstream of practice today lies in the direction of whole-bond portfolios, or core-plus.

■ *International equity.* The idea of managing whole portfolios rather than fragments has caught on in the international equity arena as well. For example, many managers now offer all-country mandates, whereas six years ago, consultants and plan sponsors had to make the allocation between two asset classes, a developed market product and an emerging market product. Once consultants and sponsors observed, however, that the periodic allocations made to developed and emerging markets were very volatile, they realized that they knew little about making an investment management allocation between these two asset classes. Consequently, many clients and their consultants have balked at making this allocation decision and have asked investment managers to make the allocation between emerging and developed markets.

Another example, which is probably more pervasive, is the increasing emphasis on industry or sector analysis in international and global equity management. As Bruno Solnik discussed, his study, along with many others, indicates that world markets (stock markets as well as economic markets) exhibit significant integration in their movements.[3] The biggest trend in international equity management during the past five years has been to reorient management approaches so that they are more in tune with the global pricing phenomenon. Interestingly, global equity and

---

[3] See Professor Solnik's presentation in this proceedings.

international equity managers with mandates that require them to invest in dozens of countries with multiple languages and currencies are succeeding; meanwhile, in the United States, consultants and clients have been led to believe that nine specialists are needed to manage a domestic equity portfolio.

Closet Indexing

The following illustration, taken from a paper I wrote with Michael Sebastian, reflects the lessons of Active Management 101 and the inefficiencies of running a closet index fund.[4] The illustration encompasses two hypothetical portfolios: one with 50 percent of its equity allocation in passive index funds and the remaining 50 percent allocation placed with eight active specialist managers and the other—an alternative whole-stock portfolio—with 80 percent of its assets in passive index funds and the remaining 20 percent with two managers who have the entire stock market as their opportunity set (i.e., managers of whole portfolios). We demonstrate that it would be reasonable to have the same level of active risk with this alternative arrangement, and if one believes that greater breadth and freedom create the opportunity for skill to excel, we would expect the information ratio of the alternative portfolio to be as large or larger than the information ratio of the 50 percent passive/50 percent active portfolio.

With this transition to the whole-portfolio alternative, a 33 bp reduction in cost occurs; that is, one can buy the same amount of active risk for about half the price. The 33 bp cost is the total cost I talked about earlier. All the elements of cost before this restructuring totaled about 65 bps, so the result is about a 50 percent reduction in the cost per unit of active risk. In this analysis, the level of active risk was maintained as constant. Most investment professionals are aware of the difference that 33 bps can make over the long run. I looked in the Russell/Mellon Analytical Services universe for total equity portfolios of large pension plans and found that a 33 bp improvement in return (the likely result of a reduction in management costs) led to a 17-percentile improvement in the 10-year universe rank of the portfolio. So, a fund at the median level could move to the top third of the universe by reducing its cost (by 33 bps) to buy the same amount of active risk—a substantial pickup.

---
[4] Richard M. Ennis and Michael D. Sebastian, "The Case for Whole-Stock Portfolios: Failure of the Multiple-Specialist Architecture." *Journal of Portfolio Management* (Spring 2001):17–26.

Conclusion

A central premise of the current multiple-specialist model is that skill is localized. The implication is that exploitable mispricings are confined to relatively homogeneous groups of stocks. If a manager subscribes to that belief, he or she need not be concerned with the whole-stock approach to portfolio management. My thesis rests on the idea that to the extent skill exists, it is not localized.

Furthermore, I do not believe that clients can orchestrate a multiple-specialist portfolio effectively. I do not think most clients have the ability to avoid misfit risk and redundancies and to effectively translate all the managers' information ratios into a single information ratio that is greater than each of the separate information ratios.

The question of the long-only constraint is another important factor in my thesis because the concepts of breadth and freedom are vital characteristics of whole portfolios. Practitioners realize that 99.9 percent of equity portfolios have a long-only constraint. It is a tradition. There are concerns about prudence and functionality, but more than one researcher has come forward with evidence that suggests that the long-only constraint has a deleterious effect on the results of portfolio management.

Traditional specialist equity portfolio managers will inevitably become increasingly aware that they are caught between a rock and a hard place. The rock—the practice of dividing portfolios into separate components with multiple managers—is a practice that has not worked for the vast majority of clients, at least those who are discerning and who analyze the performance of their portfolios carefully. The hard place will be a movement to reintegrate the equity portfolio with fewer managers and broader mandates.

Reintegrating equity portfolios in this fashion leads to the next logical question in portfolio construction: Does it still make sense to partition active equity portfolios between domestic and foreign holdings? This topic appears in much of today's research on portfolio construction. Maintaining a domestic versus foreign distinction in an efficiently managed portfolio is becoming increasingly difficult, a problem that portfolio managers of U.S. equity portfolios will have to come to terms with. This system has not been working for clients, and based on current trends in investment management, it may not work for investment managers in the future.

Question and Answer Session

Richard M. Ennis, CFA

Question: How receptive have other consulting firms and clients been to the whole-portfolio idea? From a managerial perspective, what is the available talent pool?

Ennis: I'm not aware of any other consulting firms that embrace the idea of whole-stock portfolios. Such simplification is antithetical to the interests of the industry and has a certain retro feel to it.

Yes, managers who can manage whole portfolios are available. The situation resembles the experience the industry had when it tried to find out whether any global equity managers existed. Global equity managers were around, but even though they had the capability, global management did not sell. It is a demand issue.

Nonetheless, after completing this research, we posted a questionnaire to the EnnisKnupp Web site, and within a couple of weeks, about 100 investment firms responded, asserting that they were whole equity portfolio managers. We discovered that a lot of them were not, but we wound up with a group of about 20 firms that are credible and 10–12 firms that have substantial capabilities and long track records. In fact, these 10–12 firms have been taking a whole-stock approach all along; it is the way they are organized and function. Some of those firms and products even fit into the multiple-specialist model. Most strategies fit into the multiple-specialist model, even a generalist.

So, managers, products, and capabilities (and some firms) have integrated the way they think about investing not only in the United States but also globally. A big demand for whole portfolios does not exist, however, because they are not consistent with the standard portfolio structure model.

We started using a whole-stock approach out of sympathy with our clients, who had to continually replace and hire new managers without satisfactory results. We felt that a new architecture was warranted. We're not trying to push this approach on our clients. We simply encourage them to think about it in terms of managing active risk. It embraces many different strategies, from risk controlled, so-called enhanced indexing strategies and long–short market neutral to traditional types of investment organizations, so many different types of investment management fit under this heading.

Generally, our clients are embracing the idea. They recognize the complexity of what they've been trying to do and are looking for more integrated approaches. In some sense, this concept of whole equity portfolios was just a way to bait the issue of the multiple-specialist model. Many of our clients, I suspect, will move right on to global equity portfolios because of their increasing awareness of the way financial markets are integrated.

Question: Would the use of performance fees change the cost hurdle of active management, and doesn't 50 bps in manager transaction costs seem prohibitively high?

Ennis: For an actively managed portfolio with, say, 70–80 percent turnover and one-way costs of, say, 0.75 percent, I do not know how a manager could have less than 50 bps in transaction costs. Based on data from Keim and Madhavan and others, I think it is a solid number.[1] In principle, perhaps performance fees could correct the current disadvantage in the current system of active management. Our recent paper on performance fees illustrates the differences in underlying value systems for those clients who like performance fees versus those who don't.[2] For the most part, we still see relatively little acceptance of performance-based fees on the part of clients. In looking at managers, we've always asked to see the performance-fee alternative and have encouraged our clients to consider it; in some cases, it makes sense, but I don't think it is going to be a big part of the universal solution.

Question: As a sponsor, what tolerance would you have for a whole-portfolio blowup?

Ennis: A whole-portfolio blowup is an important issue. The managers we have looked at recently who benchmark to, say, the Russell 3000 or Russell 1000 have demonstrated empirical active risk that falls about 4–6 percent around the return of the market. The potential for an unsatisfactory experience certainly exists with portfolios that have so many different ways to mess up in the short run relative to a broad market benchmark. But that does not mean that sticking with specialists against highly calibrated benchmarks is necessary. If the plan sponsors are not able to adopt a time horizon of several years in accepting underperformance against their benchmarks, they do not belong in active management. There is no way to put active management together through a multiple-specialist structure that will solve that problem. It is a significant challenge for plan sponsors. Are

---

[1] Donald B. Keim and Ananth Madhavan, "The Cost of Institutional Equity Trades," *Financial Analysts Journal* (July/August 1998):50–63.

[2] Richard M. Ennis and Michael Sebastian, "Are Performance Fees Right for Your Fund?" *Journal of Investing* (forthcoming).

they serious about trying to add value, or do they just want to appear to be going through the motions?

Question: Regarding Figure 2 and the payoff for 10 years of active management, what changed from the 1991–93 period to the 1994–98 period that might explain the dramatic drop in value added?

Ennis: Cost Effectiveness Measurement has attempted to control for benchmarks and so forth. I think that the average plan collectively had more small-cap exposure than was reflected in its benchmark. Some plans, for example, said that their benchmark was the S&P 500 Index, but they had some small-cap managers. So, the drop off in value added could be a form of misfit risk. That's my best guess. Also, many institutional investors may have been reluctant to jump on the technology bandwagon. Some prominent large-cap growth managers, for instance, did not.

Question: You discussed core-plus in fixed income as an example of whole portfolios, but these portfolios are generally seen as "opportunistic," or measured against a core benchmark, rather than adding in the "plus" and measuring against a blended benchmark. Would you comment on this practice and how it applies to U.S. equity?

Ennis: Suppose we measure core-plus portfolios against the Lehman Brothers Universal Index, which reflects the emerging markets and high-yield components. Clearly, a gaming strategy has gone on in fixed-income portfolio management, with core-plus managers being generally compared with the Lehman Brothers Aggregate Bond Index but also including these out-of-benchmark securities.

We should focus, however, on the most intelligent way to manage a portfolio in terms of creating an information ratio and then benchmark that. Doing so would reinforce the idea of the core-plus approach from a portfolio management standpoint, and it is up to the consultants and plan sponsors to ensure that the benchmark is not being gamed.

What Plan Sponsors Need from Their Active Equity Managers

Ronald N. Kahn
Managing Director
Barclays Global Investors
San Francisco

> Plan sponsors need consistent outperformance (i.e., high information ratios) from their managers. To meet this criterion, managers should use either high-breadth, risk-controlled products not unduly affected by the long-only constraint or higher-risk long–short products. Several risk-budgeting examples illustrate the attractiveness of such products.

In this presentation, I will discuss what plan sponsors *need* from their active equity managers—not what plan sponsors *want* or are currently seeking from their active equity managers. And what plan sponsors need is really not surprising.

I will begin by addressing the sponsor's perspective: What are plan sponsors trying to do? What is the investment problem they are trying to solve? A key element of this problem is understanding information ratios (IRs). Therefore, I will talk about IRs and how to achieve high IRs from an active equity manager's perspective. I will then use a few risk-budgeting examples to illustrate the plan sponsor's perspective and the way in which plan sponsors allocate plan assets to different managers. And finally, I will address how managers can continue to generate alpha in the future.

Plan Sponsor's Perspective

A sponsor hiring an active manager must balance the risk and cost of active management against its expected return. This is an optimization problem. The sponsor must choose active managers that can outperform the plan's benchmark without violating the plan's risk budget.

For example, the (fictional) Freedonia Public Employees Retirement System (PERS) domestic equity benchmark is the Russell 3000. Freedonia PERS is considering six managers. The first manager under consideration is a Russell 3000 index fund. As **Table 1** (not surprisingly) shows, the fund's alpha is zero and its active risk is 0.04 percent, close to the benchmark's performance. The second manager offers a Russell 3000 risk-controlled product with an expected alpha of 0.74 percent and active risk of 2 percent. Four traditional managers, ranging from large value to small growth, are also in the running. Note that hiring a manager whose benchmark is not the same as the plan benchmark introduces style mismatch risk in addition to active risk relative to a style benchmark.

A capital allocation analysis using Portfolio-Works (a program developed by Barclays Global Investors) produces the results shown in **Figure 1**. If the plan's risk budget is zero, the analysis allocates 100 percent of the plan to the Russell 3000 Index fund manager. As the active risk relative to the Russell 3000 benchmark increases from zero to 2 percent, the allocation to the index fund decreases (eventually to zero) and the allocation to the other active managers increases. Most plans operate in the 0.5–1.5 percent risk budget range. Plan sponsors may say that they are comfortable taking 3–4 percent risk, but in reality, taking on that much risk is almost impossible because each manager acts to diversify away the others' risk. Figure 1 shows that in the 1.0–2.0 percent range, the Russell 3000 risk-controlled product receives a significant allocation in the plan.

Why does the risk-controlled product receive such a large fraction of the plan's assets under this analysis? What drives these optimal allocations? I can address these more complicated questions by first solving a relatively simple problem—identifying the intuition governing the optimization. To do so, I assume that all managers under consideration have the same benchmark, which is the plan's benchmark,

Table 1. Example: Optimal Plan Structure, Freedonia PERS

Manager	Benchmark	Alpha	Active Risk
Russell 3000 Index	Russell 3000	0.00%	0.04%
Russell 3000, risk controlled	Russell 3000	0.74	2.00
Large value, traditional	Mostly Russell 1000 Value	1.17	4.50
Large growth, traditional	Mostly Russell 1000 Growth	1.50	7.00
Small value, traditional	Mostly Russell 2000 Value	1.01	7.00
Small growth, traditional	Mostly Russell 2000 Growth	1.02	8.00

Figure 1. Efficient Manager Allocations

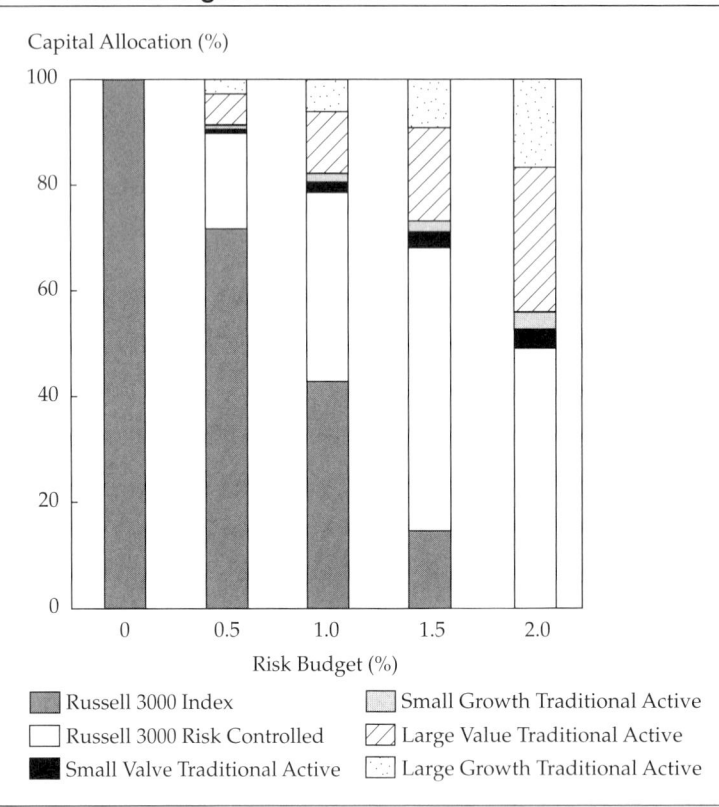

and that all active manager returns are uncorrelated. I use the following definitions to determine how to allocate a risk budget. I call the product allocation h and the risk allocation (product allocation times active risk) $h \times \omega$. So, if the sponsor allocates 20 percent of the plan to a traditional manager with 5 percent active risk, the product allocation is 20 percent and the risk allocation is 1 percent (20 percent times 5 percent). A 1 percent risk allocation means the product is contributing 1 percent to plan risk. The plan sponsor is allowing this product to consume 1 percent of the plan's risk budget.

Risk budgeting is a maximization problem: Maximize the expected alpha given the risk budget. The solution is to allocate the risk budget in proportion to IRs:

$$h_i \times \omega_i \sim IR_i = \frac{\alpha_i}{\omega_i}.$$

The risk allocation to a product should be proportional to its IR—the alpha of the product divided by its risk. The IR is a measure of performance consistency. A manager that produces a high ratio of alpha to active risk is a manager that consistently outperforms. Therefore, an optimal risk-budgeting process allocates more risk to the most consistently performing managers. If two managers have the same IR, they should have the same risk allocation. Thus, plan sponsors should allocate risk in proportion to IRs. This statement means that product allocations should be proportional to IRs divided by active risk.

Plan sponsors need high IRs from managers. This finding that sponsors are looking for managers that consistently outperform is intuitively not surprising. Thus, this analysis confirms the intuitive answer with a quantitatively rigorous explanation.

Information Ratios

Table 2 displays the results of a number of empirical studies of manager performance (for equity managers, bond managers, and institutional long-only portfolios). Based on the research, a top-quartile active manager has an IR of 0.5, which means that if the manager takes 2 percent active risk, the manager delivers 1 percent alpha, and if the manager takes 4 percent active risk, the manager delivers 2 percent alpha.

Table 2. Distribution of IRs

Percentile	IR
90	1.0
75	0.5
50	0.0
25	–0.5
10	–1.0

So, how does a manager construct an investment product that will produce a high IR? The key determinants are skill, breadth, and the long-only constraint.

Richard Grinold introduced the Fundamental Law of Active Management, which states that the IR equals the information coefficient (IC) times the square root of the breadth.[1] Remember, the IR is the ratio of active return to active risk. The information coefficient is a measure of manager skill; it is the correlation of forecasted and realized residual returns. Breadth is simply the number of independent bets per year. Thus, managers require both skill and breadth to generate a high return per unit of risk.

Skill. The easiest way to understand the concept of skill in investment management is to use a stock-picking example. I am going to define f as the fraction of an analyst's directionally correct stock-picking calls. An analyst with no skill is correct 50 percent of the time. Pure luck should produce a 50 percent accuracy rate. Perfect skill equals an f of 100 percent. The information coefficient is given by the formula $2 \times (f - 50$ percent$)$. If f is 50 percent, the IC is 0; if f is 100 percent, the IC is 1.0; if f is zero, the IC is –1. The information coefficient is thus a number between –1 and 1. Managers desire a positive number.

Breadth. To define the concept of breadth, think of the bets taken at a casino, specifically with a roulette wheel. A roulette wheel has 36 numbers; the casino wins on half of those numbers but also wins on zero and double zero. So, its odds of winning are 20 out of 38, which corresponds to odds of 52.6 percent. Although 52.6 percent does not sound like the best odds, these odds are favorable; the roulette wheel has an IC of 0.05—or $2 \times (52.6$ percent $- 50.0$ percent$)$. The roulette wheel is a great business for the casino not because of the great odds but rather because people play over and over again. If a roulette wheel takes in $20 million in bets over the course of a year, that $20 million is divided into, say, 10 million $2 bets, which translates into a lot of independent spins. If the casino instead had just one spin during the year for $20 million, the expected return would be the same, but incredible volatility would exist between winning $20 million and losing $20 million. By dividing the $20 million into a lot of small bets, the casino locks in its odds for that expected return.

A great stock picker's odds are similar to those of a casino. If a manager following U.S. equities is right 52.5 percent of the time, that manager has an information coefficient of 0.05—quite good. The stock picker, however, is not as able to achieve the same level of diversification as the casino can. Investors are often surprised to learn the low odds of good stock pickers. What drives impressive performance is the ability to diversify those odds over a large number of investment decisions. The following examples will clarify this situation.

First, suppose a manager has an IC of 0.035, which corresponds to being right about 51 percent of the time. This manager follows 200 stocks and makes new informed decisions about the stocks roughly once a quarter. This means, in effect, that the manager has a total of 800 new views on these stocks each year. The IR for this manager is 0.99 (i.e., $0.035 \times \sqrt{800}$), a top-decile investment manager. Therefore, a manager can combine a fairly low level of stock-picking ability (0.035) with a reasonably high amount of diversification (200 new stock decisions each quarter) and earn an impressive IR.

Second, consider a market timer who has an IC of 0.05. The market timer is using macroeconomic data—perhaps comparing earnings yields or dividend rates or watching the Fed—so, once a quarter, this market timer obtains new insights into whether the market will go up or down. Therefore, the number of bets per year is only four. This market timer has an IR of 0.10 (i.e., $0.05 \times \sqrt{4}$), just above the median.

Therefore, a low level of skill combined with lots of diversification yields a much better investment result than a high level of skill with little diversification.

I should caution, however, that the market-timing approach has a real benefit that these examples do not address. A market timer can outperform by 20 percent in one quarter. A market-timing strategy can thus generate huge outperformance in a short period of time, but it does not offer consistency. In contrast,

---
[1] See Richard C. Grinold, "The Fundamental Law of Active Management," *Journal of Portfolio Management* (Spring 1989):30–37.

Equity Portfolio Construction

the stock-picking approach is focused much more on generating a consistent amount of alpha.

Long-Only Constraint. Because most investors invest with a long-only product, investors must understand how the long-only constraint affects IRs. Suppose a stock picker follows a large number of stocks and ranks each on a scale from strong buy to strong sell. **Figure 2** shows that the distribution of rankings has only a few strong buys and strong sells. Most stocks rank as holds. The long-only constraint, in effect, draws a line through the distribution. The stock picker has a negative view on the stocks to the left of this line. The stock picker can neither short nor significantly underweight these stocks unless they represent a big position in the benchmark.

Figure 2. Effect of Long-Only Constraint

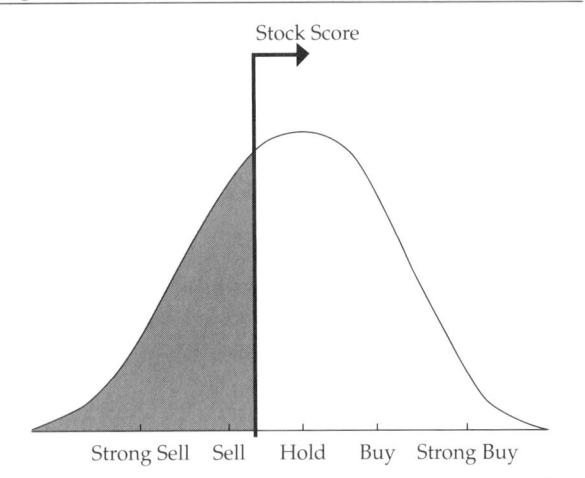

So, where should the long-only constraint line be drawn? As the line moves more toward the center of the distribution, more and more of the stock picker's information or knowledge about his or her universe of stocks will be lost because the portfolio cannot reflect this knowledge.

The key driver influencing the placement of the line is fund volatility—active risk. An investment manager increases the active risk of his or her product by increasing the overweights and underweights for individual stocks relative to the benchmark. And as the manager increases the underweights, the manager starts hitting the long-only constraint more frequently. Therefore, as active risk increases, the long-only constraint becomes more and more binding.

Ironically, the long–only constraint also hurts the manager in the stocks he or she *likes* because the overweights and underweights must balance. If a manager cannot effectively implement underweights, the manager will not be able to effectively implement overweights either. In reality, a manager can lose the ability to act on more than half of his or her information because of the long-only constraint.

Figure 3 illustrates this situation more clearly. The heavy black line is the active efficient frontier for a long-only manager. This line indicates that as a manager takes more and more active risk, the manager earns more and more alpha, but at a diminishing marginal rate. Alpha does not increase linearly because the manager starts hitting the long-only constraint. For each additional unit of risk, the manager earns less additional return.

Figure 3. Long-Only Shortfall

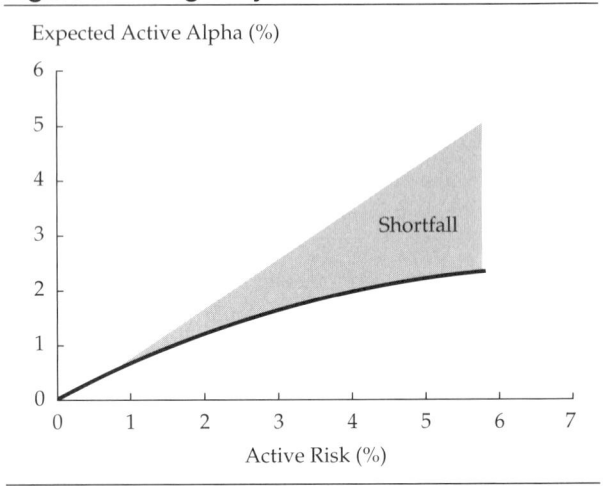

A long–short manager, however, does not face the long-only constraint. The efficient frontier for the long–short manager is the upper boundary of the gray area—a straight line. If the long–short manager is underweighting GE by 3 percent but wants to double the active risk of the portfolio, the manager can underweight GE by 6 percent. And if the manager is overweighting Microsoft by 2 percent, to double active risk the manager can overweight Microsoft by 4 percent. A long–short manager realizes a strict linear behavior in alpha, but a manager with a long-only constraint does not.

Note that at low levels of active risk, say 2 percent, releasing the long-only constraint lets the manager pick up only a little alpha. And because borrowing stocks to short them carries a cost, the additional pickup in alpha may not pay for the cost of borrowing securities at low levels of active risk. Managers, therefore, do not run long–short strategies at low risk levels. But at 5 percent active risk, which is a median level of active risk for a U.S. equity manager, the manager loses about half of his or her alpha because of the long-only constraint. Thus, once the active risk is up to 5 percent, the long–short strategies begin to dominate because of the huge alpha shortfall arising from the long-only constraint.

This shortfall can also be viewed in terms of the IR (the ratio of alpha to active risk). Referring to Figure 3, at a 2 percent active risk level, the alpha is about 1 percent and the IR is roughly 0.5. At a 5 percent active risk level, a long-only manager has about a 2 percent alpha, which is an IR of 0.4. Thus, the IR drops as risk moves from left to right in the figure. So, even though a manager's alpha will increase as the manager takes more active risk, the manager's IR will drop.

Intuitively, it makes sense that any constraint should have an impact on performance, and the empirical data in **Table 3** support this intuition. The data in the table are from the Wilshire database and show two separate universes of managers: 45 risk-controlled managers and 384 aggressive managers. Notice that the risk-controlled strategies had higher IRs for horizons greater than three years, consistent with Figure 3.

Table 3. Empirical Evidence: Top-Quartile IRs, Periods Ending December 2000

Horizon	Risk-Controlled Managers	Aggressive Managers
3 years	0.61	0.64
5 years	0.73	0.45
7 years	0.54	0.34
10 years	1.03	0.39

Note: Risk-controlled universe consists of 45 managers that state the S&P 500 is their benchmark. Aggressive universe consists of 384 top-down and bottom-up managers that state the S&P 500 is their benchmark.
Source: Wilshire Mentor Database.

Summary. Plan sponsors need consistent outperformance as measured by high IRs. Thus, from the sponsor's perspective, high-breadth, high-skill, and efficient strategies (i.e., those not unduly affected by the long-only constraint) are appealing. The best products then are risk-controlled long-only and aggressive long–short. The strategies that look least appealing from this analysis are the high-risk, long-only strategies, which are largely inefficient. This category includes concentrated long-only portfolios, which, although popular these days, combine low breadth with inefficient implementation. They certainly can generate high performance over short periods of time, but not consistent outperformance.

Risk-Budgeting Examples

Earlier in this presentation I showed that sponsors should allocate risk in proportion to IRs. In this section, I will discuss three cases of how risk budgeting works. First, I need to make some assumptions. I will consider only four products: a risk-controlled product with 2 percent active risk, a traditional and a market-neutral product, each with 5 percent active risk, and an index fund with zero risk. **Table 4** shows the characteristics of the four strategies. The traditional approach, the higher-risk, long-only product, has a relatively low IR, simply because of the inefficiency of its implementation. In fact, the highest efficiency strategy is the market-neutral product with an IR of 1. And remember, an IR of 0.5 is a top-quartile IR, so all of these IRs are good numbers. Finally, in all three cases, I assume that the plan has a risk budget for domestic equities of 1 percent. The plan's objective is to allocate to risk-controlled, traditional active, and index products to maximize plan alpha, subject to the risk budget.

Table 4. Characteristics of Sample Strategies

Product	Alpha	Active Risk	IR
Index	0.0%	0.0%	0.0
Risk controlled	1.4	2.0	0.7
Traditional	2.5	5.0	0.5
Market neutral	5.0	5.0	1.0

The purpose of the analysis is to answer three questions for each of the cases: What are the risk allocations to the risk-controlled and traditional active products? What are the product allocations to the risk-controlled, traditional active, and index products? And what is the expected alpha at the plan level?

Case 1. For this first case, I ignore the market-neutral product and assume that an IR advantage does not exist for the risk-controlled product relative to the traditional active product. This assumption is inconsistent with the previous results but serves as a good baseline case. That is, the traditional active manager and the risk-controlled manager have the same IR of 0.5 (so the risk-controlled alpha here is 1 percent, not 1.4 percent). Because I am allocating the risk pie in proportion to IRs and because the IR for these two products is exactly the same, each gets half of the risk pie. Each half of the risk pie equals 71 bps of risk because risk is not purely additive. Assuming uncorrelated active returns, plan risk is calculated by squaring each component, adding the components together, and taking the square root of the sum. Thus, the square root of 0.71 squared plus 0.71 squared equals 1 percent.

The next step is the product allocation. The product allocation equals the risk allocation divided by active risk. Because the traditional manager has 5 percent active risk, the product allocation for the traditional active product is 71 bps of risk divided by 5 percent, or 14 percent. The risk-controlled manager receives a product allocation of 35 percent of the plan—71 bps of risk divided by 2 percent—because this manager has 2 percent active risk. The product allocation to the index product is a plugged number—

the amount that allows all of the product allocations to add up to 100 percent. Therefore, because the traditional and risk-controlled product allocations equal 49 percent, the remainder, 51 percent, is allocated to the index fund. In this risk-budgeting exercise, the index fund operates similarly to cash. It is a riskless asset in this context and receives all assets unallocated in the optimization process.

The final step is to determine the plan-level alpha and plan-level IR. I know the product allocations to each of the index, risk-controlled, and traditional products, and I know the alpha of each product. The resulting alpha at the plan level is 70 bps (35 percent times the risk-controlled alpha of 1 percent plus 14 percent times the traditional alpha of 2.5 percent). Hence, the IR of the plan is 0.7 (because the active risk is 1 percent). Notice that the plan-level IR is higher than the IR of the underlying products. The reason for this improvement at the plan level is that the plan has diversified across different products; the plan adds breadth by combining managers.

Case 2. In the second case, I would like to explore my earlier assertion that risk-controlled products have an IR advantage. I will assume the risk-controlled product has an IR of 0.7 and the traditional product has an IR of 0.5. I will continue to ignore the market-neutral product for this example. If the risk-controlled product has a higher IR, it should receive a greater allocation of the risk pie. In this case, it receives 81 bps of risk. The traditional product receives an allocation of 58 bps of risk. Overall plan risk is 1 percent.

The product allocations are 12 percent for the traditional manager, 40 percent for the risk-controlled manager, and 48 percent for the index fund—adding to 100 percent.

In Case 2, the plan-level alpha is 0.86 percent, and hence, the plan-level IR is 0.86. Again, the IR of the plan is higher than that of either of the products.

Remember that in Case 1, the traditional manager received 14 percent and the risk-controlled manager received 35 percent. In Case 2, the risk-controlled product's weight in the portfolio is a bit higher than in Case 1. Thus, the lower risk level is the dominant factor driving the large allocation to the risk-controlled product. The IR advantage is a second order influence.

Case 3. In the third case, I add the market-neutral product to the product mix. Market neutral has the highest IR of the three active products. It receives the largest share of the risk pie (76 bps). Risk-controlled receives the next largest share (53 bps), and traditional receives the smallest share (38 bps).

But in the product allocations, market neutral receives only a 15 percent allocation because of its high risk. The risk budget is only 1 percent, so the amount of the market-neutral product that will fit in the plan is limited. But the inclusion of the market-neutral product lowers the allocations to the other products. The allocation to the traditional active product drops to 8 percent and that to the risk-controlled product drops to 26 percent. The index fund allocation rises to 51 percent.

The plan-level alpha (1.31 percent) and IR (1.31) are much higher in Case 3 because 15 percent of the plan is invested in a very high-alpha, high-risk product. So, even though the market-neutral product receives only 15 percent of the plan's assets, it represents the biggest risk bet and contributes the most to total plan risk. If the market-neutral product backfires, it will have a significant negative impact on the plan.

Summary. Only a few sponsors do this bottom-up type of risk-budgeting analysis. Based on my experience, however, the most useful way to instigate such an analysis is to analyze a plan's current product and risk allocations. The plan sponsor does not begin by determining what the risk budget should be but, rather, calculates the plan's current risk level. Assuming that this amount of risk is acceptable and that the plan sponsor is happy with its current managers, the analysis determines the optimal allocations to each of these managers.

I have often noticed that the allocations in existing plans tend to imply extremely high alphas for the highest risk products. That is to say, the current allocation is optimal only if the plan has extreme expectations for these products' outperformance. Often, the solution is to lower that allocation somewhat. Doing so frees up so much of the risk budget that the sponsor can shift index investments into risk-controlled products. Thus, the risk budget (total plan risk) does not change, but the manager allocations do.

Conclusion

In this presentation, I have demonstrated why plan sponsors need high IRs and how managers can successfully build products that provide them.

It is important to note that the ideas that created outperformance in the past may not work well in the future. This situation necessitates an ongoing investment in research in order to continue to generate new ideas.

To enhance the chances of outperformance, managers need to have high levels of skill, wide breadth, and efficient strategies. The investment products that look promising are risk-controlled long-only products and higher risk long–short products. But the only way these products will succeed is through an investment in research and continuing innovation.

Question and Answer Session
Ronald N. Kahn

Question: What is your definition of active risk?

Kahn: Let me describe active risk in a straightforward but technical way. Suppose I observe the performance of an S&P 500 benchmarked active equity product. It outperformed the S&P 500 by 1 percent in one year, underperformed by 2 percent the next year, and outperformed by 4 percent the following year. The standard deviation of those numbers is the product's active risk. It is a measure of how close the product performance is to the underlying benchmark.

Two percent active risk means that two-thirds of the time, the product's performance will be within two percent of the benchmark's performance. For 5 percent active risk, two-thirds of the time the product's performance will be within 5 percent of the benchmark's performance. Thus, in a given year, it would be very unusual for a 2 percent active risk product to outperform by 15 percent, but it would not be that surprising for an 8 percent active risk product to underperform by 5 percent.

Question: Do plan sponsors consider downside risk compared with upside risk?

Kahn: From a utility perspective, plan sponsors obviously want to avoid downside risk. Underperforming by 20 percent is much worse than outperforming by 20 percent.

Is there something wrong with our definition of risk? Standard deviation, which is a symmetrical definition, penalizes outperformance as much as underperformance. Is that a problem? My answer over the years has consistently been "no" for a couple of reasons. First, the products that can outperform by 20 percent can also underperform by 20 percent. So, standard deviation does a reasonably good job of finding the products that have high downside risk because they typically also have high upside risk. Second, it turns out to be difficult to accurately *forecast* downside risk.

Sticking with standard deviation has its advantages. Although downside risk formulations are intuitively appealing, they combine their appeal with a dramatic loss in accuracy in a way that is ultimately counterproductive. If plan sponsors truly cared about downside risk, they would invest in portfolio insurance or products that specifically include insurance components. Those products are not a standard component of most plans.

Question: Should a plan sponsor differentiate between two managers with the same IR but very different excess returns?

Kahn: Yes. If they have very different excess returns, they have very different risk levels. In Case 1, the two managers have the same IR, so the sponsor wants to take the same bet on each of them. That is, the sponsor wants to give each of the managers the same amount of the plan's risk budget. That means the high-alpha, high-risk product will receive a smaller fraction of the plan's product allocation, even though the two managers receive the same risk bet.

You can think about this issue in terms of individual stock picks as well. Compare a 5 percent overweight on a gas utility with a 50 bp overweight on Amazon.com. These two stock bets may correspond to the same level of active risk, but the less risky stock is the bigger active position.

Question: Do IRs in one period tell us anything about IRs in the following period?

Kahn: Unfortunately, most of the evidence shows little performance persistence. To a large extent, a product's risk level persists, so if it is a 5 percent risk product one period, it is a 5 percent risk product the next period. Looking at persistence of performance and of IRs is similar. When I have done empirical work on this topic, I have usually found slightly more positive results for persistence of IRs, but typically, the results have not been statistically significant.

Managers need to invest in research. The only way to generate future outperformance is to keep working at it, and research is a major contributor to outperformance.

Question: Does any evidence exist that IRs are higher in international markets?

Kahn: The answer depends on both the time period and the benchmark. In international markets, the average active manager outperformed consistently in the 1990s. Much of that outperformance followed from underweights on Japan. So, that outperformance would have generated higher IRs on average. If you included not only the 1990s but also the 1980s, I'm not sure you would see the same result because all the managers who underweighted Japan in the 1990s also tended to underweight Japan in the 1980s, when the Japanese market was rising steadily.

Question: If the entire industry converges to "risk control," doesn't that undermine the efficacy of the industry?

Kahn: Please don't misinterpret my presentation as an argument for low risk. There is nothing wrong with high risk. But, if you want high risk, you should use market-neutral products. In some of my examples, plan sponsors made their biggest overall bets on high-risk products as long as they had high IRs.

In the three cases I illustrated, many of the plan's assets were in the index, so there is a lot of room in principle to move out of indexing into active management. If everyone moved into indexing, that would eliminate price discovery, which would be a big problem. We need active management.

Question: If a plan is working relative to a benchmark, aren't the over- and underweighted positions equivalent to a long–short portfolio in an absolute sense?

Kahn: Yes. You can always think of your active portfolio (portfolio minus benchmark) as having long and short positions. The problem is that those positions have been restricted by the long-only constraint. So, you can always think about it as a long portfolio and a short portfolio, but the real issue is that the portfolio doesn't reflect all of your insights.

For example, if you don't like Pep Boys, which is only a fraction of 1 bp of the S&P 500, your potential underweight is very small. If you were running a long–short portfolio, however, you could be underweight 5 percent, or whatever amount you wanted. In a long-only portfolio, underweighting your active position is equivalent to being short, but in the example of Pep Boys, you're only allowed to be short less than 1 bp because that is the stock's weight in the benchmark.

Question: What's the appropriate benchmark to use for calculating the alpha of a market-neutral product?

Kahn: There are some "natural" benchmarks to use for market-neutral products. If you run a pure market-neutral product, you typically use a cash benchmark, such as LIBOR. Let's say you have $100 to convert into a long–short portfolio. With that $100, you buy $100 worth of stock and then borrow $100 worth of stock and short it, so you end up with $100 long, $100 short, and $100 in proceeds from the short sales sitting with a prime broker. Those proceeds are probably earning LIBOR minus a spread (i.e., the cost of the borrow). So, LIBOR is a natural benchmark to use in this case.

Alternatively, you can use part of those short-sale proceeds to collateralize a swap or futures overlay (e.g., an S&P 500 futures overlay). Thus, the alpha can be ported to an S&P 500 benchmark.

Question: In the example you gave for portfolio breadth, does the stock picker have to pick 200 new stocks per quarter?

Kahn: No. Think of a traditional analyst-based shop. The analysts visit companies once a quarter, or at least receive new information on the companies once a quarter. In principle, the stock picker's view on a stock could change from positive to negative roughly on a quarterly basis, and the stock picker could then implement decisions based on that view. So, the number 200 doesn't refer to 200 new stocks but 200 potentially new views based on new information.

The real question is whether all of those decisions are independent. What happens, for example, when the whole investment process uses only book-to-price ratios? The manager is essentially making a value style bet. All the manager does is rank stocks by book-to-price ratio (B/P) and then buy the high-B/P stocks. The manager may buy 200 stocks, but did this manager really make 200 independent decisions or did the manager make one decision? The technical answer is that the manager made more than one decision but not anywhere near 200. The manager does get a little diversification from one stock relative to another, but because the manager is predominately betting on one factor, the dominant effect is simply one big bet.

Question: Is the IC relatively constant over time?

Kahn: Just as the IR isn't constant over time, the IC isn't constant over time. Certain investment ideas work well over a particular period of time, and then these opportunities become arbitraged away—think of the earnings surprise effect. In the early 1990s, earnings surprises led to post-earnings-announcement drift and an investable strategy with consistent positive performance. But once everyone learned the strategy, and the *Wall Street Journal* regularly covered it, stocks began reacting within 20 minutes instead of 20 days, precluding any further profitable trading opportunities.

This is exactly why continuing research is critical for generating consistent performance into the future.

Question: Why aren't plan sponsors with long-only constraints using more risk-controlled products?

Kahn: Most plan sponsors aren't predominantly allocating to risk-controlled strategies, and by and large, they're missing a good opportunity. The rigorous analysis shows that those strategies should be a large component of a sponsor's plan.

Plan sponsors are not using risk-controlled strategies more because in doing so, they would be putting a large part of their plans into products that aren't necessarily promising the highest alphas. Plan sponsors are allocating more of their plans to the products with higher alphas.

One way to help plan sponsors better understand the issue is to say, "Let's simply reallocate your existing managers." Such a reallocation typically involves slightly reducing the allocation to the highest risk managers, which frees up so much of the risk budget that sponsors can move from index products into risk-controlled products. In the end, the plans will have exactly the same risk level but with a higher alpha.

This whole risk-budgeting exercise is not about lowering a plan's risk; it is about increasing the alpha. And the way to do that, somewhat paradoxically, is to put more plan assets into risk-controlled strategies.

Question: What should a plan sponsor do if the realized IR over a three-year period for a manager is too high?

Kahn: On the one hand, we would all like to have that problem. But on the other hand, are the manager's risk controls appropriate? Say a manager was hired with the expectation that he or she was going to deliver X and instead delivered $3X$. Was the payoff so big because the manager made a big bet that you didn't know the manager was taking?

As a plan sponsor, I would try to understand where that extra performance came from. Is it a bet that could turn around and just as likely result in negative performance in the future? Does the manager understand his or her own investment process, and will the process be managed properly in the future?

The Role of Benchmarks in the 21st Century

Howard M. Crane, CFA
Watson Wyatt Investment Consulting
Seattle

> Benchmarks are central to portfolio construction, particularly to the asset allocation, risk budgeting, and performance measurement processes. Although no single role exists for benchmarks, choosing benchmarks wisely allows plan sponsors (or other investors) to distinguish skilled managers from lucky ones and to structure the total portfolio as efficiently as possible.

My presentation has three main subjects: benchmark functions in the asset planning cycle, portfolio structure and risk control, and an integrated solution for risk budgeting. Benchmarks are central to all of these topics. The main task in the 21st century will be the development of a thoughtful approach to the overall problem of portfolio construction and risk management. Although the principle of Occam's razor suggests that the simplest possible solution to a problem is generally the right one, I agree with Einstein, who said, "Everything should be made as simple as possible, but not simpler." Making things simple, but not too simple, is precisely the challenge of dealing with benchmarks.

Benchmark Functions in the Asset Planning Cycle

The asset planning cycle is a process with eight stages:
- mission and governance,
- risk budget mandate,
- risk budget allocation,
- strategic asset allocation,
- benchmark design,
- asset-class structure development,
- manager selection, and
- plan monitoring and change.

The starting point of the asset management challenge for the institutional investor is defining the mission and the governance structure of the fund to be managed. Next, a board of directors, or some group of fiduciaries with oversight responsibilities, must identify how much risk will be taken in the management of plan assets. The important thing to note is that this decision is about determining the *total* amount of risk that can be taken by a fund and then allocating the risk among various investment opportunities though a process of strategic asset allocation, benchmark design, asset-class structure development, manager selection to fill in the skeleton of the structure, and finally, appropriate control and revision procedures for the management of plan assets. The asset planning cycle should be a closed loop and a continuous process.

Asset Allocation Foundation. Asset allocation is the foundation for using benchmarks. Asset allocation is based on deciding how much risk to take in search of a return objective, whether that return objective is stated only in terms of assets, in terms of asset risk and return opportunities, or (as we at Watson Wyatt believe is proper) in terms of both assets and liabilities in combination. I view the pension management problem as a spread business. The central task is managing the spread between the assets and liabilities. So, deciding how much plan risk to take is essentially the decision of how much risk to take relative to the plan's asset/liability spread, which is either a surplus or a deficit.

The process of implementing asset allocation combines a number of different asset classes into a portfolio whose expected return and risk offers the highest likelihood of meeting investor objectives within the acceptable level of risk that was defined in the initial risk budget. In implementing asset allocation, each asset class is represented by an index benchmark, which effectively captures the investment characteristics of the complete market opportunity.

Investable benchmarks allow passive investment at a very low cost. All asset-class structural decisions are based on departures from the benchmark index. Investors with sizable assets can invest in a benchmark for less than a basis point, but added value really comes from betting away from the major indexes. When using benchmarks in asset allocation and in portfolios, if the benchmark is flawed, all elements of the asset planning cycle will be affected, from the asset allocation decision through the performance measurement decision. So, understanding benchmarks and using them effectively is a real key to investment success. Perfect benchmarks do not exist. They all have flaws and range along a spectrum from good to bad or better to worse.

Historical Perspective. Thirty years ago, when stock-level and fundamental data were hard to get, indexes were composed of "representative" stocks. That is, for example, the DJIA, S&P 500 Index, and MSCI Europe/Australasia/Far East (EAFE) Index were representations of the market as a whole. The various index providers at the time used sampling methodology to structure their indexes. The early indexes had a number of things in common; for example, the composition of the indexes was essentially controlled by committee. In fact, the indexes were managed—actively in some cases—and subjective judgment was often used to supplement the rules of index construction. As technology and data capture have improved, indexes have evolved away from the early sampling structure and toward more complete market structures.

In 2002, indexes offer multiple representations of the same markets. For example, the U.S. equity market can be represented by the Russell 3000, Wilshire Total Markets, or S&P 1500 Supercomposite index. All index providers will try to make a case that supports why their index is better than their competitors'. But because all indexes are flawed in one direction or another, some guidelines are helpful in choosing among them. Different benchmarks have differences in weightings by virtue of their construction, and although they may represent the same market over the same period of time, they actually represent different realized returns and risks. Of course, anyone who has been running index funds or measuring performance using the S&P 500 knows that there are about 14 different returns for the S&P 500, each of which can be argued is methodologically right or methodologically wrong, depending on the speaker's viewpoint. So, picking the return that serves the plan's purpose best is an interesting game that all managers of index funds have at least considered, if not played.

All index providers today create subindexes for style groups and capitalization tiers. The key question for portfolio construction is whether the subindexes sum to the aggregate in terms of the asset allocation decision without building in misfit risk or tracking error.

Choosing a Benchmark. Choosing a benchmark involves making decisions based on several key trade-offs:
- *Availability of investable proxies, subject to the cost of managing them.* Index fund managers know that managing to a Russell index, for example, requires heavy turnover (as much as 60 percent, depending on recent activity in the market) at reconstitution time.
- *General acceptance by managers and performance evaluators.* Credibility of a particular index is enhanced if it is already in widespread use by other investors and performance measurers.
- *Ease of communication.* Index benchmarks must have a makeup that is easily explained to the users of the benchmarks, whether they are trustees, senior governing fiduciaries, operating fiduciaries, or participants in a defined-contribution plan.
- *Quality and timeliness of data.* Because frequent monitoring of actual versus policy allocation is a necessary requirement for many investors, timely and accurate pricing and composition information are critical. These data are required so that the fund manager can manage his or her portfolio efficiently and so that performance can be readily monitored.
- *Stability of structure.* Predictability of index structure is essential if assets are to be managed in a manner consistent with the benchmark. Minimizing performance drain by minimizing transactions makes stability a key criterion for selection. Turnover within the index should be kept to a minimum, and changes should be clearly understood. Furthermore, changes in the construction rules should not occur frequently so that the future construction of the index is projectable.
- *Minimizing misfit with the chosen portfolio structure.* Sub-asset-class index components should be chosen to most closely resemble the normal habitat of the managers they benchmark while summing to the desired asset-class aggregates with minimum misfit.

Regardless of the trade-offs that a plan sponsor or manager faces when choosing an appropriate benchmark, the characteristics of a best-practices benchmark are well defined. They are low cost, unambiguous, investable, and measurable. In addition, a best-practices benchmark should have data integrity, known constituents, assignment fit, broad coverage, and an institutional presence.

Future of Indexes. As I mentioned, the spectrum of indexes runs from better to worse. Traditional capitalization-weighted indexes have some real failings. They are subject to bias caused by overstatement of investable float and are characterized by volatility from changes in P/E multiples associated with the cap weighting. Thus, cap-weighted indexes do not maximize return to risk. Index construction schemes other than cap weighting can improve investment efficiency, which I define as the "information" or "return-to-risk" ratio. If stocks are homogeneous statistically and highly correlated, the risk–return relationship will be the same regardless of the weighting methodology. So, cap weighting makes a good deal of sense in a market that is essentially homogeneous. If correlations are low, however, equal weighting produces the maximum amount of risk (i.e., variance) reduction.

Perhaps, then, the ideal structure for an index would be equal weighting for all sectors and cap weighting within those sectors. This approach is a logical way to proceed because it produces the most efficient portfolio and index in risk–return terms. And this observation presents an interesting opportunity for improving investment efficiency in portfolio construction and portfolio measurement. The few investors who choose to structure a proprietary benchmark for their portfolios with a scheme other than cap weighting will almost certainly capture an economic profit—a "pioneer's premium"—by following the path that diverges from the path chosen by most of the rest of the world. Accordingly, a number of investment management firms are in the process of developing unique approaches to benchmark and portfolio structure.

Peer Groups and Normal Portfolios. Peer group comparisons are now viewed, particularly in the United States, as secondary measures and an inferior tool for benchmarking performance. Even in Europe, the last bastion of peer group measurement, the trend away from peer group comparisons is growing. Likewise, normal portfolios (customized benchmarks that include all the securities in a manager's universe of choice, weighted as the manager would weight them in a portfolio), at least in our experience, are no longer widely used. They fail some of the tests of a good benchmark that I noted earlier in that they are difficult to create and both their concept and composition are difficult to communicate to users. The normal portfolio is not particularly stable; rather, it is a moving target that changes as the manager's investment opportunity set changes. And the use of normal portfolios tends to force undue focus on offsetting misfit versus the benchmark, although misfit may not actually be the problem. Indeed, misfit that is compensated for by high returns is desirable.

In fact, in my view, a cap-weighted index is the ultimate peer group. To the extent that most sponsors and managers use these representations of their habitats, they are all competing closely with the same average—one which by virtue of transaction costs and fees they are likely to underperform.

Portfolio Structure and Risk Control

The primary goal of portfolio structure is to capture the risk and return characteristics of an asset class chosen in strategic asset allocation. The asset class should be represented by a fully diversified and investable index. For example, U.S. equities may be represented by the Russell 3000 or S&P 1500 Supercomposite index. The next objective is to add active return to the index by using active management in a way that departs from the index. In seeking active return, the investor must accept active risk, which means moving away from the benchmark; active management produces active return—always. The only question of interest is whether the active return is positive or negative. Of course, the challenge for all portfolio managers is capturing a positive active return.

The portfolio structure decision requires the answers to two questions: How much active risk should be taken in the portfolio, and how should that risk be taken? To answer those questions, managers have to identify the right level of risk for each client, identify the risks with the best return prospects, and most importantly, remove the risks from the portfolio that are poorly rewarded. In determining the portfolio structure, these principles are important for deciding what to do actively and what to do passively. The goal is to build a portfolio structure that maximizes financial efficiency—the net information ratio (as described by Ronald Kahn[2])—and is capable of practical implementation within the manager's and sponsor's governance structure.

For example, the core–satellite approach is widely used by institutional investors. As shown in **Figure 1**, a core portfolio, whether it is an index fund, an enhanced indexed fund, or a low-risk broad core

---
[2]See Mr. Kahn's presentation in this proceedings.

Figure 1. Example of Core–Satellite Approach

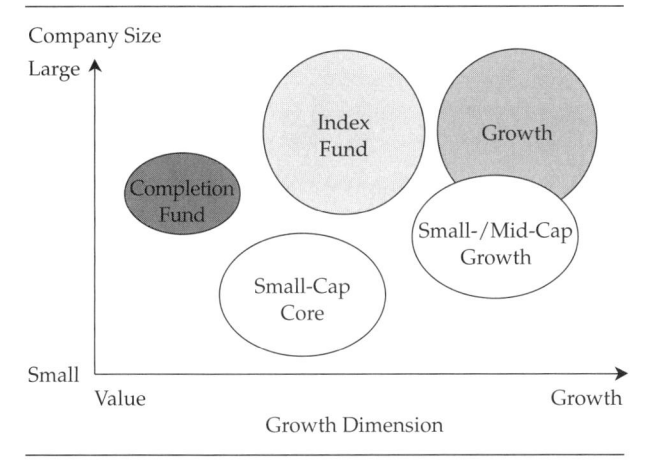

portfolio, is supplemented by a variety of portfolios with different management styles, capitalization tiers, and value or growth orientations. Regardless of the approach, the resulting portfolio structure will differ from the asset-class benchmark, resulting in misfit, and the amount and direction of misfit will vary with the structural choices made by the manager. Misfit can be optimized, however, and offset with appropriate "completion" index funds. If the alpha of the structure is great enough, misfit risk will be compensated. Misfit and risk level must be managed; it is simply a question of who will do it.

A benchmark facilitates the effective delegation of risk mandates and the measurement of comparative performance. The benchmark—one that all parties concerned can follow and use as an appropriate reference point—is used to delegate the risk mandate to a plan's managers. The particular assignment given to a manager should dictate the choice of benchmark, and the benchmark should be a fair and effective discriminator of active management skill. In the 1970s and early 1980s, many managers sought to be measured relative to the S&P 500, which allowed them to successfully game the index by investing outside the index and to "earn" a performance-based fee as a result, although much of the outperformance was attributable to luck as frequently as it was to skill. Thus, the right benchmark can aid in distinguishing luck from skill and effective managers from charlatans. A desirable benchmark minimizes the opportunity for passive gaming and minimizes the opportunity for managers without skill to charge a skill-based fee. Also, the correct benchmark should facilitate the measurement of sources and magnitudes of risk so that active risk can be decomposed and attributed to asset allocation and other active decisions.

Risk Budgeting: An Integrated Solution

Benchmarks are needed as a schematic for portfolio design and as an effective tool for performance measurement. Ultimately, successful portfolio construction is the product of a total, integrated solution known as "risk budgeting." Risk budgeting is the process of determining the amount of total investment risk to be spent on an investment program and the allocation of the risk among different areas of investment opportunity, taking into account the governance of the program, the financial requirements of the program, and the attractiveness of various risk–reward opportunities and their interrelationships.

For example, **Figure 2** looks like any other efficient frontier, but it is based only on active risk and return. (The index fund represents zero active risk and zero active return.) The active opportunities are shown as either active satellite managers or active core managers. Clearly, satellite managers tend to take more risk than core managers. In structuring the portfolio, one can build moderate-active-risk portfolios and higher-active-risk portfolios by varying the types of managers used and the allocations given to each. The risk level and return opportunities of each manager—determined by the respective manager—are chosen by the plan sponsor to target a given level of return at a given level of active risk.

In terms of risk budgeting, many structures are possible within a particular asset class, and the choice

Figure 2. Risk Budgeting

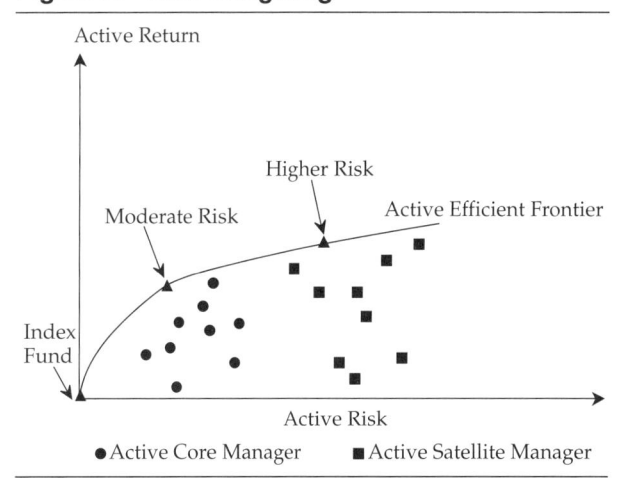

Note: Moderate risk: index fund = 25%; enhanced index = 40%; active 1 = 10%; active 2 = 15%; active 3 = 10%.

Higher risk: index fund = 0%; enhanced fund = 20%; active 4 = 30%; active 5 = 35%; active 6 = 15%.

Source: Based on data from Barton Waring, Duane Whitney, John Pirone, and Charles Castille, "Optimizing Manager Structure and Budgeting Manager Risk," *Journal of Portfolio Management* (Spring 2000):90–104.

of structure is based on a variety of factors, such as client risk tolerance, strengths and weaknesses of the various managers in the opportunity set, benchmark deviation (tracking error) of the chosen managers, costs of implementation, client belief sets, and governance preferences. The structure decision indicates two things: the confidence level (high or low) that an exploitable investment opportunity exists and the confidence level that the plan sponsor has in being able to successfully capture the opportunity in implementation. Ultimately, the structure, from a risk management standpoint, depends on the potential deviation from the benchmark by the active managers, remembering that the satellite active managers have greater benchmark deviation than do the core active managers.

Although building active structures that appear to have a successful risk–return profile is easy, the associated costs of those structures may be extremely high. I am always mindful of the fact that the portfolio manager gets paid first with certainty and the client gets paid next with uncertainty. As Richard Ennis points out, the more costs are reduced, the higher the fund owner's confidence will be in capturing added value.[3]

What Makes a Good Structure? The governance budget, the kind of resources used in making portfolio structure decisions, should match the risk budget. When more risk is taken, more governance is needed to manage the risk effectively. A good structure (the right level of risk or tracking error) meets the needs and preferences of clients and avoids unintended bets. It also avoids bets that are relatively inefficient in terms of their risk–reward ratio.

A good structure maximizes financial efficiency by employing high-confidence managers, maximizing the expected net information ratio, and diversifying risk among the most volatile management styles so that neither the total portfolio nor the asset-class portfolios are subject to the vagaries of the same macro themes. A problem in global-balanced mandates—for example, multiple assignments and multiple asset classes run by a single firm—is that the decisions about those asset classes are almost always governed by a central policy authority, and the result tends to be a similar set of macro risks embodied in all of the different asset classes.

Nonfinancial efficiency is intrinsic to building a good portfolio structure. Nonfinancial efficiency is essentially the "sleep-well factor"—the belief that the structure is strong and will not subject the client to regret risk great enough to question staying the course. Nonfinancial efficiency means avoiding a structure that is over-engineered and that has a governance model incompatible with client belief sets.

The strategic asset allocation, benchmark design, and manager structure and selection decisions are the products of the interaction of the risk budget and governance budget. The requisite outputs of the entire process are the financial payoffs (investment returns) and the nonfinancial payoffs (comfort on the part of the fiduciaries in the decision-making process and resulting portfolio structure).

Structure Goals. A portfolio's structure defines the characteristics of the portfolio, such as risk, reward, and financial efficiency, relative to the portfolio's benchmark. "Risk" is defined as the tracking error relative to the benchmark. "Reward" is defined as the excess return above the benchmark return, in other words, alpha. "Financial efficiency" is defined as the reward per unit of risk, in other words, the net information ratio—that is, Net IR = [(Alpha – Fees and implementation costs)/Tracking error]. So, measuring investment efficiency effectively requires the right benchmark, one that eliminates noise, luck, and gaming opportunity for the manager. And all of the factors should be considered in the context of the nonfinancial efficiencies (comfort and compatibility with client belief sets) and practicality (the governance budget).

Completing the Risk Budget. As I noted earlier, the risk budget should address two questions: How much total portfolio risk should be taken, and where in the portfolio should that risk be taken to optimize return? Those questions should be answered (or, in other words, the risk budget should be defined) relative to some measure of the liabilities that the asset portfolio is designed to settle or defease. The appropriate measure varies, but market-based measures of pension plan liabilities, such as Statement of Financial Accounting Standard (SFAS) No. 87 or International Accounting Statement (IAS) No. 19, have certain merits, such as marking the true financial risk of the investment plan to market. The key asset/liability (A/L) measures used in risk budgeting, however, are total returns versus liabilities (A/L returns) and the standard deviation of A/L returns (A/L risks). The point is that return and risk should not be assessed in asset space alone but in A/L space, which harkens back to my earlier point that the spread between assets and liabilities is an important factor in the amount of risk that a portfolio should take. To complete the risk budget, the investment policy and implementation strategy must be defined so that allocations to asset classes and managers can be decided as shown in **Exhibit 1.**

---

[3] See Mr. Ennis's presentation in this proceedings.

Exhibit 1. Inputs Needed to Complete the Risk Budget

Item	Percentage Allocation	Detailed Specification
Policy	Asset classes	Index
Implementation	Manager types	Mandate

Size of the Risk Budget. In general, the size of the risk budget is contingent on the relationship of the pension fund to the sponsor. The relationship has four main elements—covenant, maturity, surplus, and risk beliefs:

- *Covenant.* The stronger the covenant of the employer/sponsor to meet the future funding requirements of the retirement plan, the more risk that can be taken in managing the assets of the pension fund.
- *Maturity.* The longer the funding period and the term of the plan's liabilities, the more risk that can be taken in managing the fund without compromising the security of final benefit payments.
- *Surplus.* The larger the current funding excess, or cushion (current assets minus liabilities), the more risk that can be taken in the fund.
- *Risk beliefs.* The stronger the risk preferences or return beliefs of the client (the subjective view of the plan's trustees about risk and return), the more risk that can be taken in the fund.

Finding the Integrated Solution. Five progressive steps align the asset allocation process with the risk allocation process. The process begins with the most basic of allocations—that between bonds and stocks—and ends with an assessment of the total improvement in the expected information ratio arising from the strategic enhancements to the portfolio as compared with the expected information ratio of the baseline strategy. The allocation decision in each step is analyzed based on the trade-off between A/L return and A/L risk or tracking error. Liabilities are stated in an SFAS No. 87 context. In the analysis that follows, I will be comparing the improvement in asset return and the increase in tracking error of various portfolios relative to the minimum risk portfolio (a duration-matched AA corporate bond portfolio). (Steps 1 through 4 are independent, and Step 5 combines the preceding four.)

▪ *Step 1: Equities versus bonds.* The first step is the allocation between equities and bonds, as shown in **Figure 3**. The minimum risk opportunity at the far left of the efficient frontier (100 percent bonds) is an AA corporate bond portfolio with a duration equal to the duration of plan liabilities. For most plans, the total duration of liabilities is four to seven years longer than the longest AA corporate bond in the market. So, in practice, the bond allocation exhibits

Figure 3. Example Risk Budget: Equities versus Bonds

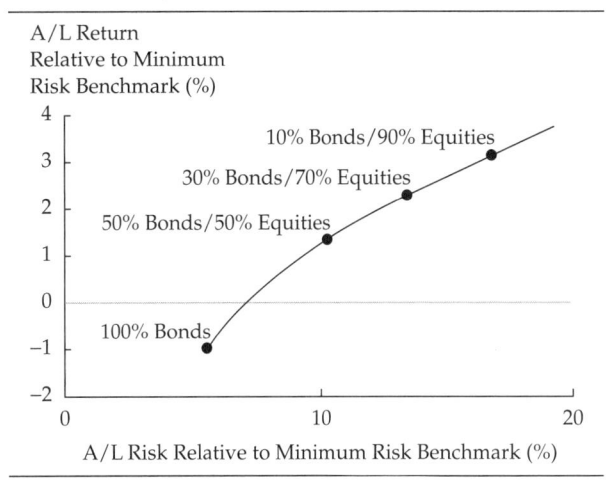

Note: Minimum risk benchmark is AA bond.

misfit from the zero-risk position and is the reason why the 100 percent bond allocation (the minimum-risk portfolio) is associated with a –1 percent A/L return and positive tracking error. Misfit risk is that portion of the efficient frontier that crosses and falls below the horizontal zero line. Along the efficient frontier, the equity/bond allocation of the efficient portfolios gradually shifts from 100 percent bonds (the minimum-risk opportunity) to 100 percent equities (the highest-risk opportunity). An asset allocation decision is reached based on the factors noted previously—risk tolerance, time horizon, governance, and nonfinancial efficiency.

▪ *Step 2: Equity allocation.* Once the allocation is made between equity and nonequity, the next step is the allocation decision within the equity portfolio—for example, domestic versus nondomestic, as shown in **Figure 4**. In this case, the baseline strategy is 70 percent U.S. equity and 30 percent foreign equity—a

Figure 4. Example Risk Budget: Equity Allocation

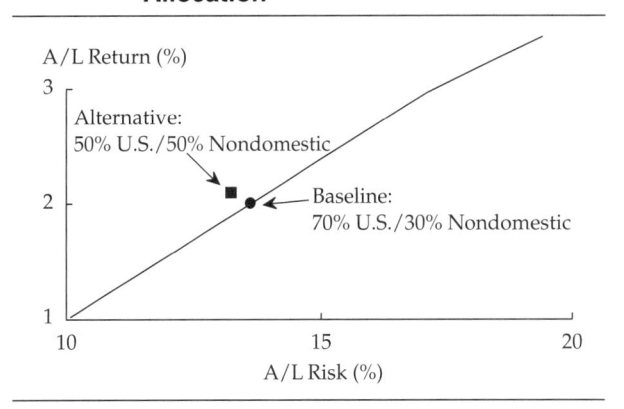

Equity Portfolio Construction

mix that most U.S. asset allocation modeling identifies as efficiency maximizing. In most U.S. pension fund asset allocations, by contrast, the nondomestic allocation is 20–21 percent of the total equity allocation, a somewhat less financially efficient mix that gives the typical fiduciary more nonfinancial comfort. The baseline allocation offers an expected information ratio of about 14.9 percent, which is the expected return divided by the expected tracking error of that return. When the ratio of foreign to domestic stock is increased, the risk–reward trade-off is improved. The point just above the efficient frontier represents a 50/50 U.S./non-U.S. equity allocation. This allocation has a slightly higher expected return and, by virtue of the diversification benefit, a slightly lower risk; the information ratio of the alternative strategy is 15.6 percent. The lower correlation between U.S. and non-U.S. equities generates the improvement in risk relative to the A/L benchmark. The goal is to improve investment efficiency, and in this case, the risk budget supports more foreign diversification.

■ *Step 3: Alternative assets allocation.* With the U.S./non-U.S. equity allocation made, the next decision is, within the equity asset class, whether to use alternative equity assets, as shown in **Figure 5**. Based on a 70/30 U.S./non-U.S. baseline strategy, adding 5 percent to alternative investments—for example, hedge funds and private equity—and lowering the listed U.S. equity allocation from 70 percent to 65 percent will increase the return and, by virtue of diversification, will also reduce aggregate portfolio risk. This change improves the information ratio of the alternative strategy, shifting it from 14.9 percent, the information ratio of the baseline strategy, to 16.9 percent. Clearly, the risk budget supports alternative assets.

Figure 5. Example Risk Budget: Allocation to Alternative Assets

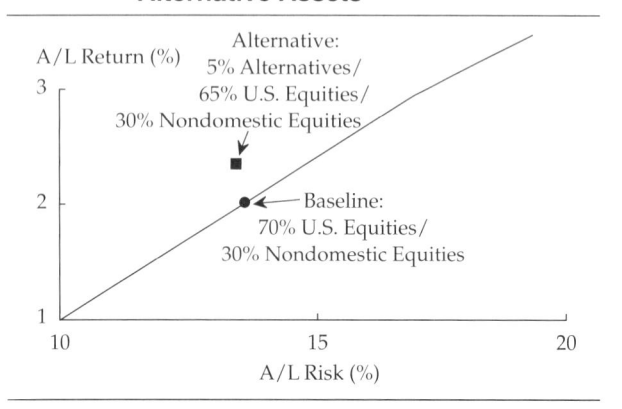

■ *Step 4: Policy and implementation risks.* The next step is to decide the optimal allocation between active management and passive management, as shown in **Figure 6**. The interior set of axes represents manager risk and return relative to the policy benchmark—in other words, framing the decision in terms of a departure from a pure asset allocation with investable benchmarks and into potential active management. In this case, moving to active management improves return but it also incurs some benchmark deviation risk, some tracking error. To view this trade-off in isolation, as many plan sponsors have been doing in recent years, is to focus solely on the increase in active risk without considering the impact on total portfolio risk. In my view, because active management risk and asset allocation risk are essentially independent, the inclusion of active management risk increases total portfolio risk only slightly. As shown in Figure 6, using good active management improves on the baseline information ratio of 14.9 percent, increasing the information ratio for active implementation to 16.3 percent. Again, the risk budget supports good active management.

Figure 6. Example Risk Budget: Policy and Implementation Risks

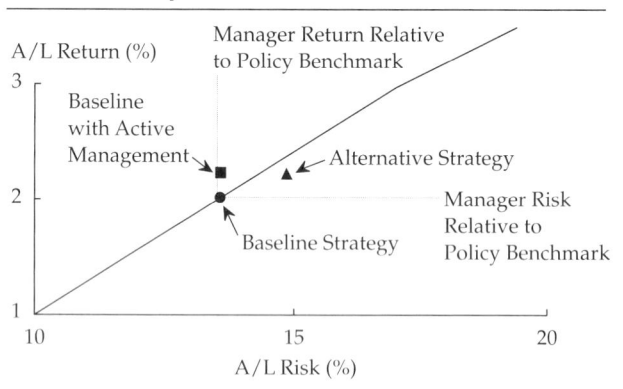

■ *Step 5: Strategic enhancements.* Finally, when all the strategic enhancements to the portfolio are combined, as shown in **Figure 7**, the information ratio moves from 14.9 percent to 19.0 percent. Return increases, and the aggregate risk in A/L space is reduced in an SFAS No. 87 context by virtue of the diversification of four relatively uncorrelated strategies. The various return components of the portfolio structure are additive, but the risks are not because the various risk allocation decisions tend to be minimally correlated. Thus, departing from the index benchmark by using different style elements in a total portfolio context confers an advantage in terms of the risk–return trade-off.

Figure 7. Example Risk Budget: Combination of Strategic Enhancements

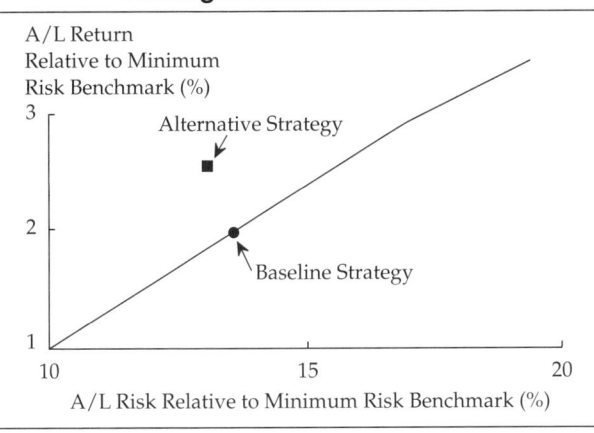

A/L Return Relative to Minimum Risk Benchmark (%) vs. *A/L Risk Relative to Minimum Risk Benchmark (%)*, showing Alternative Strategy above the line and Baseline Strategy on the line.

Optimal Risk Bets. In allocating the risk budget, the overall contribution to the information ratio should be the prime determinant of where risk should be taken. Ultimately, that directive begs the question of whether most risk should be taken in asset allocation or in active management and alternative investment strategies, and that decision is, in turn, very much driven by confidence in the assumptions used in the portfolio construction process, as well as the client's belief sets. In most cases, confidence levels are higher for asset allocation inputs and much lower for active management and alternative investment risk and return assumptions. This greater confidence in estimates is one key reason why plan sponsors tend to spend most of their risk budgets on asset allocation (the preceding Steps 1, 2, and 3) and less on implementing active management (Step 4).

Consistent with the goal of allocating risk to improve the information ratio is the goal of allocating risk (fixing and implementing policy) in line with the governance budget used in the management of the fund. The fund sponsor may operate with a low, moderate, or advanced governance budget. The sponsor may want an extreme active management contribution, but if the plan has a low governance budget, the sponsor should limit risk allocations to credit, the bond benchmark, and/or the equity benchmark. As the willingness to expend the governance budget increases, the sponsor can move the fund's risk allocations into absolute return mandates, barbell structures, and cash equalization to maximize the investment opportunity set. A moderate governance budget encompasses risk allocations to alternative assets and to currency and specialist managers and requires periodic rebalancing.

The components of an integrated solution to portfolio construction are as follows. First, the strategic asset allocation is made to bonds, equities, and alternatives. Next, benchmarks are designed for the specific characteristics within each overarching asset allocation. The active/passive, core/satellite, and absolute return mandates are then decided, and manager selection is completed. Each component has an investable benchmark, or in the case of absolute return or alternative assets, has a comparator—some vehicle for measuring performance but one that is not investable. Each component has a measurable and separable contribution to investment efficiency improvement.

In summary, the superior model for managing portfolio structure and risk allocation decisions is to evaluate the fund in a consolidated manner, including asset allocation and active management, so that all investment-related risks can be viewed on a common platform; essentially, policy risk and implementation risk are the same thing. The prioritization of decisions can be effected within a risk-budgeting framework by analyzing an asset's marginal contribution to the improvement in the information ratio and the investment efficiency of the portfolio. The governance budget is a key differentiator between pension funds and constrains the amount of risk that can be taken.

Conclusion

The continued evolution of markets and benchmarks will keep the fund management process highly dynamic over time. Indexes are not perfect benchmarks, but they are reasonable proxies for the investment opportunity set. The good news is that the mathematical measurements are just fuzzy enough to require the use of judgment, and with the appropriate judgment, the result will be an effective answer. If benchmarks are chosen wisely, skilled managers can be distinguished from the lucky ones.

Managers seek to maximize the value of benchmark risk arbitrage—in other words, gaming—so their behavior will change as their benchmarks change. As benchmarks continue to evolve, investment managers will struggle to find opportunities for outperformance.

In structuring the total portfolio, expanding the investment opportunity set essentially allows funds greater potential to improve their situation, but it also makes the job of risk assessment more uncertain. Every portfolio structure should be managed to exploit the possibilities for continuous improvement through broadening the parameters of the investment opportunity set, which means the portfolio structure must be modified over time. Therefore, ongoing adjustments to the total amount of acceptable portfolio risk and to the way that risk is allocated within the portfolio are required—with recognition that the governance budget dictates the risk budget.

The role of benchmarks in portfolio construction does not lie solely in the numbers. In fact, no single answer, or role, exists; rather, a set of alternative appropriate answers exists, the selection of which depends on the criteria demanded of the benchmark. Various structural alternatives for benchmark and portfolio construction can be tested quantitatively, but ultimately, the problem is one of forecasting future risk and return opportunities, both of asset classes and managers within them. This forecasting process requires judgment and some sort of adjunctive qualitative appraisal.

Question and Answer Session

Howard M. Crane, CFA

Question: Why aren't there more equally weighted indexes? And why isn't there a natural benchmark misfit if managers are prone to equal weighting and benchmarks are cap weighted?

Crane: First of all, not much research has focused on this idea of homogeneity versus heterogeneity, so there haven't been a lot of very useful and widely publicized ideas for using an equal-weighted benchmark. And the indexes in the public domain were originally all cap weighted. Managers equal weight because, in many cases, they think that all of their ideas potentially have equal value. They diversify by dollar, not by risk. Does it guarantee a misfit if a portfolio manager equally weights a portfolio and it is measured by a cap-weighted benchmark? Absolutely.

We have a benchmark measurement that is offered up as essentially a cap-weighted scheme, and portfolio managers are given the opportunity to either follow it or move away from it. Managers are actively undertaking this question as a business problem for themselves rather than for their clients, in terms of how much deviation risk they are willing to tolerate from the benchmark. Taking huge amounts of risk is discouraged as a business strategy, and in the use of cap-weighted indexes, equal-weighted portfolios tend to be extreme performers.

Because of their structural differences from the cap-weighted benchmarks, equal-weighted portfolios perform extremely well or dismally. Is the right answer to switch to an equal-weighted benchmark? If the plan sponsor is willing to define the investment opportunity set in that context, a switch is a great idea. If not—if the plan sponsor wants a proxy for the true investable universe—the sponsor is going to pick a cap-weighted benchmark.

Question: Could you compare and contrast the use of benchmarks versus peer group universes in terms of the relative efficacy for evaluating managers?

Crane: The problem with peer groups is that they are not investable, are not defined in advance, and are unstable. For more information on this, I recommend to you an article by Jeff Bailey in the CFA candidate readings.[1]

Question: Could you give some pros and cons about customized benchmarks?

Crane: I take this question as a reference to normal portfolios—structuring a benchmark that exactly proxies the no-information starting point for a given manager. I think normal portfolios are an extraordinarily good idea for discriminating between skill and luck

---

[1] Jeffrey V. Bailey, "Are Manager Universes Acceptable Performance Benchmarks?," *Journal of Portfolio Management* (Spring 1992):9–13.

or skill and gaming. So, for the narrow purpose of effectively managing the manager, if the governance budget is large enough to do it, normal portfolios are great. Unfortunately, they tend to be expensive, are difficult to explain, and have a lot of misfit. The typical response is to turn the crank on the optimizer to minimize the misfit. But if you improved investment efficiency enough in terms of adding alpha, you would be disposed to accept misfit. Normal portfolios, then, are clearly the best way to measure managers, but they're not necessarily the best way to manage to an aggregate asset class and are a very expensive way to manage to a total portfolio structure that has multiple sources of misfit.

Question: Could benchmark gaming be a skill in its own right?

Crane: Benchmark gaming is definitely a skill, but the question is whether the client should be paying for it. Consider the Lehman Aggregate Bond Index as the benchmark for the bond market. The Lehman Aggregate Bond Index encompasses only 50 percent of the bond market. So, as a manager, if I'm reasonably insightful, I can take some credit risk and a little convexity, stir in a little duration, and lo and behold, I can beat the benchmark in my sleep before I actually have to think about making hard decisions. This is an example of gaming that can be solved by better defining the benchmark to measure the market.

Innovations in Risk Measurement

Mark P. Kritzman, CFA[1]
*Managing Partner
Windham Capital Management Boston
Cambridge, Massachusetts*

> Three innovative ways of attacking the management of risk at the portfolio level are to include within-horizon risk, to consider the effect of short selling on the lognormality of returns, and to acknowledge the greater importance of security selection over asset allocation in the production of wealth (returns) and happiness (utility). Three lessons emerge. First, whether measuring risk as the probability of loss or value at risk (VAR), investors need to measure *continuous* risk. Second, whenever a portfolio manager takes short positions (even if only by varying from the benchmark), VAR will be underestimated. Third, security selection is much more important than asset allocation in terms of the dispersion in cumulative returns.

This presentation about risk management, although at times couched within the context of hedge funds, extends to virtually every investment situation. Delving into the issue of risk management requires a look at how analysts actually measure risk versus how they *should* measure risk, as well as a look at the age-old question of whether asset allocation or security selection has greater potential to influence performance. My "modest proposal" at the end provides a "*dispositive*" solution, a possible final settlement, to this question.

How Should Risk Be Measured?

The traditional risk measures need to be recast to clarify that an investor's exposure to loss occurs not only at the end of the investment horizon but also throughout the investment period. To demonstrate this fact, I will ignore many of the familiar mismeasurement problems—fat tails, estimation error, and so on—by assuming that this is a perfect world with perfect markets, that fund returns are independently and identically distributed (i.i.d.), and that everything is transparent. Thus, for purposes of this presentation, I assume that the means, variances, and correlations of security returns can be estimated with certainty. I will demonstrate that in this perfect world, investors are exposed to much more risk than traditional risk measures reveal. And when the problems I am assuming away are introduced, the result is that the risk is even greater than what I am describing for the perfect world.

Inadequacy of Standard Risk Measures. Analysts typically think about risk in one of two ways—probability of loss and value at risk (VAR). Probability of loss is estimated by applying the normal distribution function to the difference between the targeted loss amount and the expected return, divided by the standard deviation of return:

$$\text{Probability of loss} = N\frac{\text{Percentage loss} - \text{Return}}{\text{Risk}}.$$

Because I assumed i.i.d. returns, everything must be converted into continuous units to allow use of the normal distribution. So, in standardized units,

$$\text{Probability of loss} = N\frac{\ln(1+L) - \mu T}{\sigma\sqrt{T}}, \quad (1)$$

where

- $N[\bullet]$ = cumulative normal distribution function
- $\ln$ = natural logarithm
- L = cumulative percentage loss in periodic units
- μ = annualized expected return in continuous units
- T = number of years in horizon

[1] This presentation is based on joint work with George Chow, Sebastien Page, and Don Rich.

σ = annualized standard deviation of continuous returns

Note that Equation 1 gives the calculation for the probability of loss at the end of the investment horizon.

VAR is the flip side of the coin. VAR is an estimate of the amount the investor might lose at a given probability. Again, because of compounding and the subsequent use of the normal distribution, I use continuous units, so the formula for VAR is

VAR = (Return − Normal deviant × Risk)(Portfolio value)

or

$$\text{VAR} = -(e^{\mu T - Z\sigma\sqrt{T}} - 1)P, \qquad (2)$$

where
- e = base of the natural logarithm (2.718282)
- Z = normal deviate associated with the chosen probability
- P = portfolio value

This type of risk measurement is common in the investment industry. For example, suppose you have an investment of 100 (of some monetary unit) that has an 8.55 percent expected return and a standard deviation of 12 percent. You want to calculate the likelihood of a 10 percent or greater loss as of the end of one year. To calculate probability of loss and value at risk, you first convert the 8.55 percent to its continuous counterpart, which is 7.6 percent, and do the same with the standard deviation, which makes it 11.02 percent. Then, you plug these numbers into Equation 2. You find that the probability of a 10 percent loss as of the end of one year is 5 percent. With e = 2.71828, Z = 1.645 (5 percent), and P = 100.00, Equation 2 produces a VAR of 10.

Measuring Continuous Risk. The incompleteness in the typical risk analysis is that the risk pertains only to the end of the investment horizon. I am going to invoke the words of a famous economist, John Maynard Keynes, to argue that investors need to care about what happens along the way to that horizon. Many investors are no doubt familiar with Keynes' famous aphorism "In the long run, we are all dead." But what they may not know is that this (rather trite) sentence is only part of a longer, eloquent statement that makes the point I want to make:

> In the long run, we are all dead. Economists set themselves too easy, too useless a task if in tempestuous seasons they can only tell us that when the storm is long past the ocean will be flat.[2]

This statement is profound. Investors need to survive storms, but if they measure risk as only what can happen at the end of the storm, they ignore anything that might happen during the storm.

■ *Probability of loss.* **Figure 1** illustrates this idea of within-horizon risk. Suppose you have an investment that has an initial value of 100 and it could follow five possible paths over four periods. You want to estimate the likelihood of a 10 percent loss. Analysts typically look at the ending distribution to see how many of the paths are below 90. Figure 1 indicates that only one path is below 90 at the horizon date. So, a typical analysis would conclude that the likelihood of a 10 percent loss is 20 percent, or one in five. This approach fails to account for the fact that of the four paths that end above 90 at the horizon date, three cross the 10 percent loss threshold along the way. So, the probability of a 10 percent loss, if you care about what happens at all during the period prior to the horizon date, is not 20 percent but 80 percent. This definitional difference is big, and it is not unusual.

Figure 1. Risk of 10 Percent Loss: Ending Wealth versus Interim Wealth

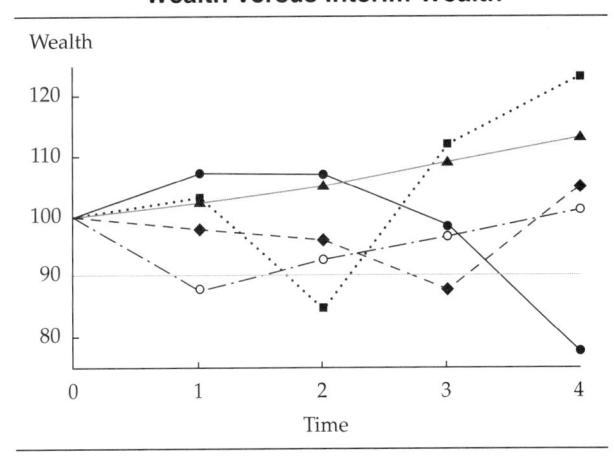

To account for the within-horizon risk, a new formula is needed:

$$\text{Probability of loss} = N\frac{\ln(1+L) - \mu T}{\sigma\sqrt{T}} + (1+L)^{2\mu/\sigma^2} N\frac{\ln(1+L) + \mu T}{\sigma\sqrt{T}}. \qquad (3)$$

Note that the first part of Equation 3 up to $(1 + L)^{2\mu/\sigma^2}$ is Equation 1. So, the first part of this formula is the probability of loss at the end of the investment horizon, and a second term is added for probability of within-horizon loss (a term that is always greater than zero). The result is a formula that gives the probability of loss throughout the investment period, including at the end.

---
[2] From *A Tract on Monetary Reform* (1923).

This same approach can be used to establish a new measure of VAR, which I call "continuous VAR." Suppose you want to know the probability of a 10 percent loss during the holding period. The approach tells you, assuming you value the investment continuously, whether the value is expected to drop 10 percent below the beginning investment value at any point throughout your investment period. Whereas conventional VAR tells you, for a given probability, the worst that can happen at the end of the investment horizon, continuous VAR reveals, for a given probability, the worst that can happen at any point within the investment horizon.

Within-horizon risk is important because many managers, analysts, and investors need to be aware of certain threshold losses that could occur throughout the investment period. It is particularly important for hedge funds, which need to remain solvent.

Figure 2 shows the difference between end-of-horizon and within-horizon risk measured over a 16-year period. The horizontal axis represents the length of the investment horizon in years. An investment is made at the beginning (Year 0) and is valued at periodic intervals (starting with Year 0.25) during a 16-year period. An 8.55 percent expected return and a 12 percent standard deviation are assumed. The bottom line plots the probability of losing 10 percent as of the end of the quarter, the end of six months, and so on for the next 16 years. After about two years, the probability of a 10 percent loss at the end of the horizon starts to fall and gradually approaches zero. This line represents the notion of time diversification—that is, the longer the investment horizon, the less likely an investment will suffer a given loss.

The middle line in Figure 2 represents the likelihood that the investment will lose 10 percent at some time within the horizon but will recover by the end of the horizon. The top line is the probability of a 10 percent loss at the horizon's end but also within the horizon. That is, it shows the probability that the investment will lose 10 percent in value at some point within a quarter, within six months, within eight years, and so on. In other words, the top line is the sum of the other two lines.

Two important messages should be obvious from this figure. The first is that the probability of loss within the horizon is much higher than the probability of loss at the end of the horizon. The second is that within-horizon probability of loss is not lowered with time; it increases. It will never turn down. If an investor cares about what happens to an investment's value from the first day the investment is made until the end of the investment period, then the longer the horizon, the greater the probability of loss.

This message has implications for the time diversification debate. The idea held by proponents of time diversification is that risk is diversified by the passage of time; that is, investors should be willing to take more risk over longer horizons than over shorter horizons. On the opposing side is a famous paper by Paul Samuelson in which he showed, given random returns and constant relative risk aversion, that investors should not change their attitude toward risk as time increases.[3] Yes, as the horizon extends, the likelihood of a loss at the end of the horizon diminishes, but the amount that can be lost increases, and under certain kinds of utility functions, those two outcomes exactly offset each other. Samuelson's argument depended on the notion of the magnitude of loss. But the paths in Figure 2 do not depend on the magnitude of loss to argue the fallacy of time diversification. Never mind the magnitude of loss; the likelihood of loss—if one cares about what happens along the way—always increases. Time is not necessarily an ally.

Consider a numerical example involving a hypothetical hedge fund. This hedge fund imposes on its investors a three-year lockup period. Now, suppose the manager of the hedge fund buys a three-year U.S. T-note with an expected return of 3.5 percent and a standard deviation of 3 percent. Next, the manager engages in an overlay strategy to enhance return. This overlay strategy has a 4 percent expected return and a 5 percent standard deviation, and the overlay returns are independent of the T-note return. **Table 1** shows the expected return and standard deviation of the hedge fund with various amounts of leverage (for example, "Leverage 2×" means 2 times net asset value). Given this information, what is the likelihood of a 10 percent loss with each of the various levels of

Figure 2. Components of First Passage Risk
(8.55% return, 12.00% risk)

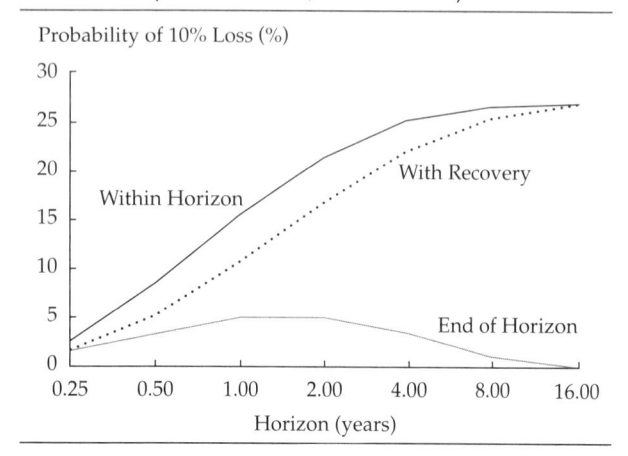

---
[3]Paul A. Samuelson, "Risk and Uncertainty: A Fallacy of Large Numbers," *Scientia* (April/May 1963):1–6.

Table 1. Return and Risk of Increased Leverage

Measure	Underlying Asset	Overlay Strategy	2×	4×	6×	8×	10×
Expected return	3.50%	4.00%	11.50%	19.50%	27.50%	35.50%	43.50%
Standard deviation	3.00	5.00	10.44	20.22	30.15	40.11	50.09

Leverage of Overlay Strategy spans the 2× through 10× columns.

leverage? **Figure 3** provides the likelihood of a 10 percent loss, as analysts typically measure it, as of the end of the three-year period and within the three-year period. With leverage of 2, the probability is very low that this fund will have depreciated by 10 percent or more by the end of three years. Even with leverage of 10, the probability of a 10 percent loss at the end of the horizon is still quite small.

Figure 3. Probability of 10 Percent Loss: Three-Year Horizon

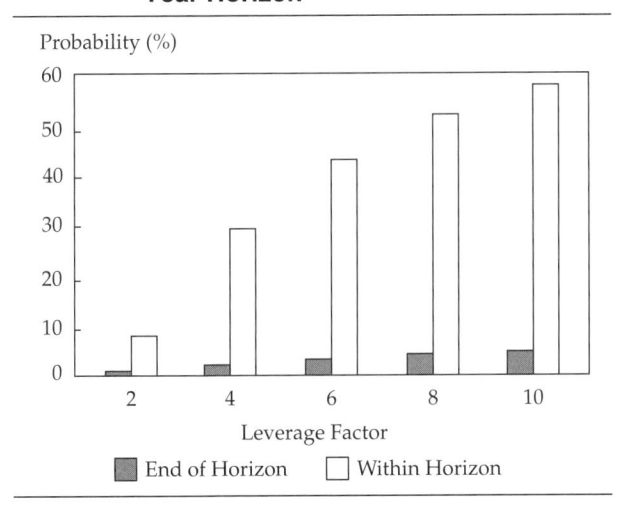

This kind of analysis may (falsely) reassure hedge fund managers and investors that high amounts of leverage are not a problem and may thus encourage them to increase the amount of leverage that they use. But what is the likelihood that this fund's value will be down 10 percent or more at some point during that three-year horizon (the lockup period)? As Figure 3 shows, this likelihood is much greater than the end-of-horizon probability of loss.

The point is not that hedge fund managers should not use leverage, that hedge funds are too risky, or that investors should be more conservative. The point is that investors and managers ought to be aware of the probabilities of loss throughout the investment period, not just at the end of the period.

■ *VAR.* A similar comparison of within-horizon (continuous) and end-of-horizon (conventional) risk of loss can be done for VAR analyses. **Figure 4** shows the difference in the risks at a 5 percent confidence level, a three-year horizon, and different amounts of leverage. With leverage of 2, the conventional VAR is negative. That is, the worst outcome at a 5 percent confidence level is actually a small gain. In fact, for every amount of leverage, the conventional VAR is very low. In contrast, for every amount of leverage, the continuous VAR is much higher than the conventional VAR. For example, with leverage of 10, a 5 percent probability of within-horizon loss represents about 45 percent of the fund's value.[4]

Figure 4. VAR (5 Percent Confidence Level): Three-Year Horizon

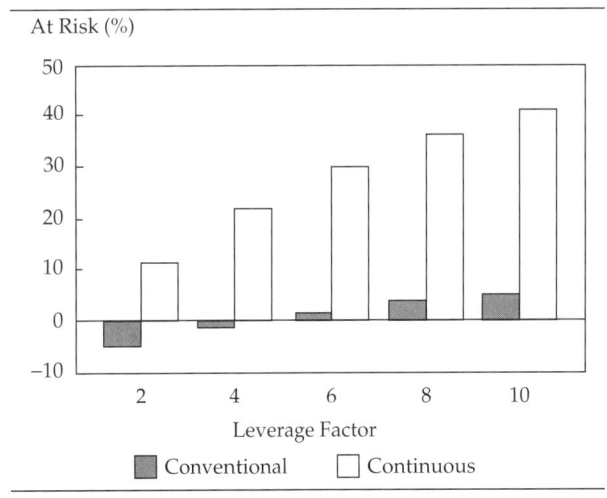

Effect of Short Positions on VAR. For this portion of my analysis, I assume the same perfect world (markets are perfect, transactions are transparent, and parameters can be estimated with certainty), except that instead of the fund returns being i.i.d., the returns of the individual assets that make up the funds or the portfolios are i.i.d. This discussion will clarify why, when I measure VAR a certain way, I underestimate VAR when the portfolio has short positions but not necessarily when the portfolio has long positions.

The issue is as follows. If I assume that the portfolio's individual asset returns are i.i.d., the process of compounding causes the distribution of the

---
[4] For more on continuous measures of risk, see Mark Kritzman and Don Rich, "The Mismeasurement of Risk," *Financial Analysts Journal* (May/June 2002):91–99.

returns to be lognormal. The distribution is skewed to the right. The assumption of lognormality at the portfolio level is a good approximation of the true distribution of a long portfolio. When the portfolio contains short positions, however, lognormality is not a good approximation.

The issue is particularly relevant for long–short and market-neutral hedge funds and every long portfolio that is measured relative to a benchmark. By definition, such a portfolio is short the benchmark through overweighting some positions and underweighting others. So, if relative performance is important, the assumption of lognormality at the portfolio level will significantly understate VAR. This finding can be explained by the Central Limit Theorem and the effect of compounding on lognormality.

■ *Central Limit Theorem.* First, consider what I call "the poor person's proof of the Central Limit Theorem." The Central Limit Theorem is the notion that the distribution of the sum or average of independent random variables that are not individually normally distributed will approach a normal distribution if the number of variables is large enough. This reality is ubiquitous in mathematics and in nature. My favorite example of a normal distribution is the geyser Old Faithful in Yellowstone National Park. If many eruptions are observed, the time intervals between eruptions will be normally distributed.

What follows is the poor person's proof of the Central Limit Theorem. Panel A in **Figure 5** shows the distribution of the toss of a single die. It is called a "uniform" distribution because all of the outcomes have an equal probability. **Table 2** shows the possible outcomes if two dice are thrown together. There is only one way to get a 2, only one way to get a 12, six ways to get a 7, and so on. If I plot the probabilities shown in the right-hand column of Table 2, they produce a distribution that is no longer uniform. It has a peak at seven, as shown in Panel B of Figure 5. Panel C shows the distribution of the outcomes of tossing 1,000 dice together, which is very close to a normal distribution. Thus, many things in nature and math are normally distributed.

■ *Lognormality in returns.* A pattern that investors would prefer to be normally distributed is asset returns. Unfortunately, they are not; they are lognormally distributed. The following explains why. Suppose an investor has an investment that has only two possible outcomes in a one-year period—it can go up 25 percent or down 5 percent—and these outcomes are equally probable. If the expected return over one period is 10 percent (that is, a 50 percent chance of a +25 percent return and a 50 percent chance of a –5 percent return), then at the end of two periods, the

Figure 5. Distributions

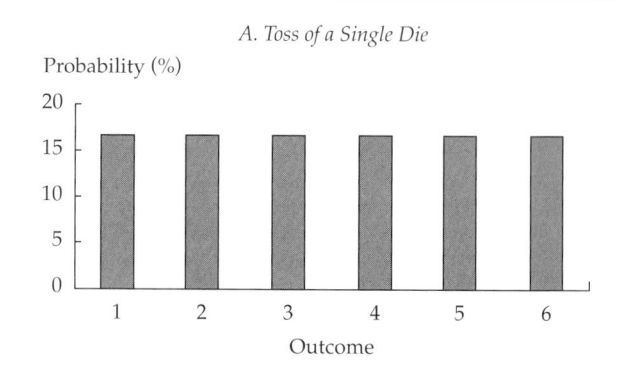

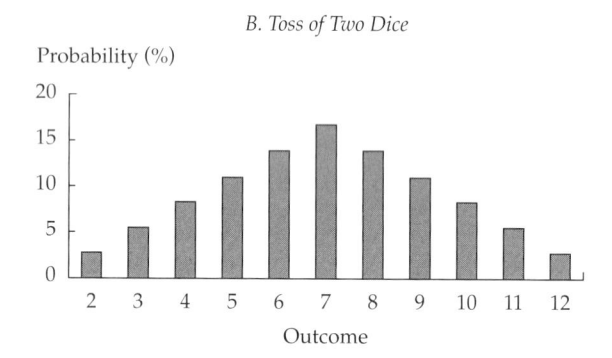

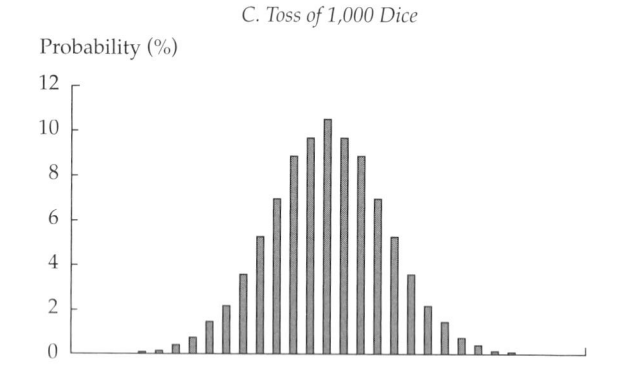

A. Toss of a Single Die

B. Toss of Two Dice

C. Toss of 1,000 Dice

Table 2. Results of Tossing Two Dice

Outcome	Possible Combinations	Probability
2	1–1	2.78%
3	1–2 2–1	5.56
4	1–3 3–1 2–2	8.33
5	1–4 4–1 2–3 3–2	11.11
6	1–5 5–1 2–4 4–2 3–3	13.89
7	1–6 6–1 2–5 5–2 3–4 4–3	16.67
8	2–6 6–2 3–5 5–3 4–4	13.89
9	3–6 6–3 4–5 5–4	11.11
10	4–6 6–4 5–5	8.33
11	5–6 6–5	5.56
12	6–6	2.78

returns can follow four possible paths: up 25 percent twice in a row, which produces a 25 percent probability of earning 56.25 percent; up 25 percent in the first period and down 5 percent in the second period or vice versa, both of which produce a 25 percent probability of an 18.75 percent return; or down 5 percent twice in a row, for a 25 percent probability of a –9.75 percent return. The average of those four cumulative returns is 21.00 percent, which is the same as 10 percent compounded over two periods.

Consider this pattern more closely. **Table 3** shows four return sequences in which the asymmetry in possible returns for this investment is clear. In the "cumulative periodic returns" column, the average value is 21 percent. If the return is up 25 percent twice in a row, the result is a return of 35.25 percentage points (pps) above the average return of 21 percent; if the return is down twice in a row (–5 percent each period), the cumulative return is 30.75 pps below the average return of 21 percent. The next set of columns converts these periodic cumulative returns to continuous cumulative returns. For example, a 56.25 percent periodic return in continuous units is 44.63 percent, which means that a 44.63 percent continuously compounded return increases an investor's wealth by 56.25 percent. The differences from the average cumulative continuous return (17.19 percent) of 44.63 percent and –10.26 percent are exactly symmetrical: Each differs 27.44 pps from the average. In short, periodic returns are asymmetrical, and if the investor repeated this investment over many periods, the investor would observe a lognormal distribution. Continuous returns, however, are exactly symmetrical, and if the investor repeated this investment over many periods, the continuous returns would be normally distributed.

■ *Fitted versus simulated risk.* The next step is to examine how these patterns affect VAR. If an investor is long in an investment, VAR is measured by the left tail of the distribution of the investment's returns, and the distribution is skewed to the right. Note that lognormality is good because bad outcomes are not as bad as good outcomes are good. For example, if the investment is up 10 percent twice in a row, the investor is up 21 percent, but if the investment is down 10 percent twice in a row, the investor is down only 19 percent. For this reason, VAR under lognormality is lower than if the distribution is normal.

The problem arises when the investor is shorting an investment. In this case, the investor's worry is the *right tail*. Just as compounding helps when an investor is long, it hurts when the investor is short. In this case, if the investment is up 10 percent twice in a row, the investor is down 21 percent. So, when a manager adds short positions and long positions together, the VAR that comes from a lognormal distribution will be biased. It will understate the true VAR.

A simple example shows exactly by how much VAR will be understated. Suppose a manager has a portfolio divided equally between two assets, long positions in both stocks and bonds, and each has the return, risk, and correlation given in **Table 4**. Assuming for the moment that the returns at the portfolio level are lognormal (whereas it is known that the individual assets' returns are lognormal), the fitted distribution is as shown by the continuous line in **Figure 6**. Now, consider the following simulation. Assuming that stocks individually and bonds individually are lognormal, I draw 50,000 return pairs to generate a simulated return distribution by using Monte Carlo simulation. These return pairs are represented by the bars in Figure 6. Note the region in the left tail that is of concern regarding VAR; little difference exists between the fitted distribution and the simulated distribution.

Table 4. Security Characteristics for Long-Only Portfolio

Characteristic	Stocks	Bonds
Expected return	10.00%	8.00%
Standard deviation	20.00	10.00
Correlation of stocks and bonds		30.00%

The simulation is the truth in this example, whereas the analytical solution, the fitted line, is the false approximation. But if the manager is long, whether or not the analytical solution is used matters little. The assumption of lognormality at the portfolio level for a long portfolio is a good approximation.

But what happens when the manager uses short positions? Suppose the leverage is two times—that is, the portfolio is short 100 percent bonds and long 200 percent stocks. **Figure 7** shows the fitted distribution (assuming portfolio lognormality) and simulated (true) distributions in this case. The fitted

Table 3. Four Return Patterns: Lognormal Distribution

	Periodic Returns		Continuous Returns	
Return Sequence	Cumulative Return	Difference from Average	Cumulative Return	Difference from Average
25%, 25%	56.25%	35.25 pps	44.63%	27.44 pps
25%, –5%	18.75	–2.25	17.19	0.00
–5%, 25%	18.75	–2.25	17.19	0.00
–5%, –5%	–9.75	–30.75	–10.26	–27.44
Average	21.00%		17.19%	

Equity Portfolio Construction

Figure 6. Fitted versus Simulated VAR: Stocks 50 Percent, Bonds 50 Percent

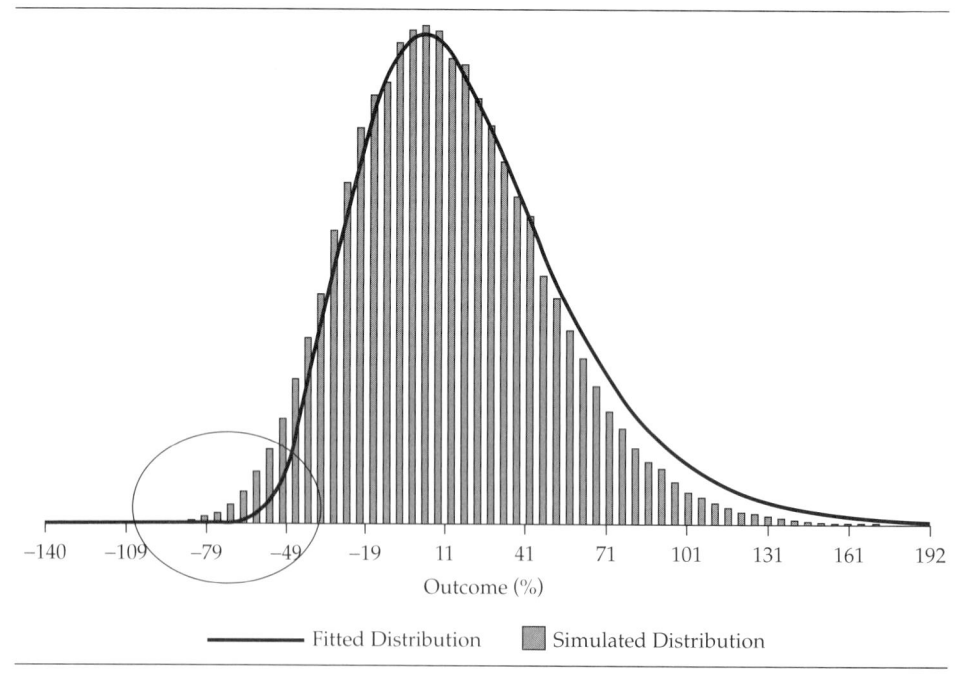

Figure 7. Fitted versus Simulated VAR: Long Stocks 200 Percent, Short Bonds 100 Percent

distribution is greatly displaced toward the right, which indicates that the manager is significantly underestimating VAR.

Now consider a strategy in which the manager does a pairs trade. The two assets are depicted in **Table 5.** Asset A has a low expected return, and Asset B has a high expected return. They have the same risk

Table 5. Security Characteristics for Long–Short (Pairs Trading) Portfolio

Characteristic	Asset A	Asset B
Expected return	5.00%	30.00%
Standard deviation	40.00	40.00
Correlation of A and B	50.00%	

and are 50 percent correlated. Suppose the manager goes short Asset A because of its lower expected return and goes long Asset B because of its higher expected return. **Figure 8** shows the fitted distribution and the simulated distribution. Again, the left tail (VAR) is underestimated; the misestimation is obvious.

Table 6 shows the actual amount of underestimation of VAR for several portfolios ranging from a long-only combination of half stocks and half bonds to the pairs trade that I just described. The fitted and simulated VAR for each is given for a 5 percent and a 1 percent cutoff. Note the difference between the VAR for the 1 percent cutoff when lognormality for the pairs trade is assumed (47.57 percent) and for the true VAR (77.69 percent). It is a huge difference. This issue is thus important, and managers and investors need to be aware of it.

Asset Allocation versus Security Selection

I am going to change direction now and address the question: What is more important—asset allocation or security selection? The received doctrine is that asset allocation is more important. This belief gained empirical support in 1986 with a paper by Brinson, Hood, and Beebower.[5] The authors conducted performance attributions on 91 pension plans to determine how much of the plans' returns were the result of the long-term asset-mix policy, deviations from that asset policy mix (timing decisions), and security selection. When they ran a regression of the total returns on these component returns, they discovered that 93.6 percent of the return variation through time depended on the asset policy mix; the rest depended on timing and stock selection.

But in my view, interpreting this result to mean that asset allocation is more important than security selection is wrong. The problem (and it applies to many other types of studies) is that the study did not disentangle the opportunity set from investor behavior.

The Brinson et al. study actually tested a joint hypothesis: What opportunities were available in the capital markets at the time, *and* what investment activities did investors choose to perform? The study did not measure which is more important but what investors actually did. And what investors did was to put the bulk of their emphasis on asset allocation.

---

[5]Gary P. Brinson, L. Randolph Hood, and Gilbert L. Beebower, "Determinants of Portfolio Performance," *Financial Analysts Journal* (July/August 1986):39–44.

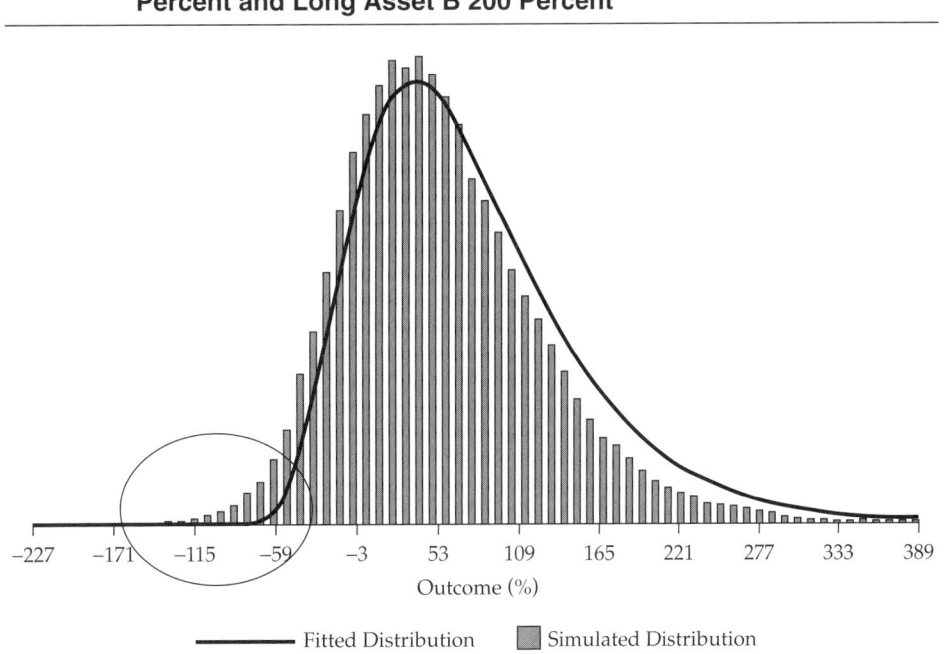

Figure 8. Fitted versus Simulated VAR: Pairs Trade with Short Asset A 100 Percent and Long Asset B 200 Percent

Table 6. Fitted versus Simulated VAR Results for Various Portfolios

	5% Cutoff		1% Cutoff	
Portfolio	Fitted	Simulated	Fitted	Simulated
Stocks/Bonds				
50/50	10.20%	10.02%	16.90%	17.13%
–50/150	29.50	31.58	40.79	45.05
–100/200	38.58	44.53	51.01	62.79
Asset A/Asset B[a]				
–100/200	29.87	42.25	47.57	77.69

[a] Assets as specified in Table 5.

Brinson et al. measured the performance of 91 large corporate pension plans. Each of those plans had several active equity managers, and each of those active equity managers was running a fund with, probably, little tracking error. So, the researchers were taking the average returns of all of those funds, with the result that the tracking error, on average, was close to zero. Indeed, no security selection was going on at these funds. Never mind whether security selection was important or not; it simply was not being done. Therefore, this study says nothing at all about the relative importance of asset allocation and security selection, but the industry did not interpret the study in this way.

In a study I conducted with Sebastien Page, we specifically attempted to disentangle investor behavior from the importance of asset allocation relative to security selection.[6] Following are some of our findings.

Defining Importance. We defined importance as the extent to which a particular activity causes dispersion in wealth (in cumulative returns) or dispersion in investor happiness (utility). Dispersion is important to investors who possess skill or believe they can acquire skill because it allows them to increase wealth beyond what would occur from passive investment or from average performance. So, if an investor is skilled, dispersion makes the investor richer. For investors who do not have skill, dispersion is just as important, however, because it exposes them to losses that might arise as a consequence of bad luck.

Logically, one might think that security selection is more important because individual securities far outnumber asset classes and because individual securities are more volatile than the asset classes that encompass them. The only way asset allocation would be more important is if the individual securities were highly correlated with one another within the asset classes and if the correlations between asset classes were low. So, the relative importance of securities and asset classes is an empirical question: Which is the dominant effect—the higher volatility of individual securities or the higher correlation between the individual securities within the asset classes?

To find the answer to this question, Page and I began with a simple mathematical model of relative importance. Equation 4 measures the volatility of the return differences between two assets, which is sometimes called tracking error:

$$\sigma\varepsilon_{A1,A2} = (\sigma_{A1}^2 + \sigma_{A2}^2 - 2\rho\sigma_{A1}\sigma_{A2})^{1/2}, \quad (4)$$

where

$\sigma\varepsilon_{A1,A2}$ = relative volatility between Asset 1 and Asset 2
σ_{A1} = standard deviation of the returns of Asset 1
σ_{A2} = standard deviation of the returns of Asset 2
ρ = correlation between Asset 1 and Asset 2

Equation 5 shows the volatility of an asset class that encompasses two assets:

$$\sigma_A = \left[\left(\sigma_{A1}^2 \times 0.5^2\right) + \left(\sigma_{A2}^2 \times 0.5^2\right) + (2\rho\sigma_{A1} \times 0.5 \times \sigma_{A2} \times 0.5)\right]^{1/2}. \quad (5)$$

With this information, we can calculate the tracking error between asset classes, which is:

$$\sigma\varepsilon_{A,B} = (\sigma_A^2 + \sigma_B^2 - 2\rho\sigma_A\sigma_B)^{1/2}, \quad (6)$$

where

$\sigma\varepsilon_{A,B}$ = relative volatility between Class A and Class B
σ_A = standard deviation of Class A
σ_B = standard deviation of Class B
ρ = correlation between Class A and Class B

Example of Trade-Offs. Suppose an investor has two asset classes and each class has within it two securities. **Table 7** shows the relative volatility—the potential for dispersion and thus the measure of importance—for various standard deviations of the securities and correlations between the securities and between the asset classes. Panel A assumes that the volatility is the same, 10 percent, for each of the four securities (A1, A2, B1, and B2) and the securities are

---

[6] Mark Kritzman and Sebastien Page, "Asset Allocation versus Security Selection: Evidence from Global Markets," Revere Street Working Paper Series, Financial Economics 272–279 (February 2002).

Table 7. Simple Mathematical Model of Relative Importance

	Standard Deviation	Correlation of the Two	Relative Volatility of the Two
A. All correlations equal zero			
A1	10.00%		
A2	10.00	0.00%	14.14%
B1	10.00		
B2	10.00	0.00	14.14
A	7.07		
B	7.07	0.00	10.00
B. All correlations equal 50 percent			
A1	10.00%		
A2	10.00	50.00%	10.00%
B1	10.00		
B2	10.00	50.00	10.00
A	8.66		
B	8.66	50.00	8.66
C. Asset class correlation equals 33.3 percent			
A1	10.00%		
A2	10.00	50.00%	10.00%
B1	10.00		
B2	10.00	50.00	10.00
A	8.66		
B	8.66	33.33	10.00
D. Asset class correlation equals 25 percent			
A1	10.00%		
A2	10.00	50.00%	10.00%
B1	10.00		
B2	10.00	50.00	10.00
A	8.66		
B	8.66	25.00	10.61

uncorrelated. Under those assumptions, each asset class (A and B) has a standard deviation of 7.07 percent. The findings for relative volatility indicate that the choice of security is more important than the choice of asset class; the relative volatility between the two securities within the asset classes is 14 percent, whereas the relative volatility between the asset classes is 10 percent.

Panel B shows the results of the calculations when the correlation between both the securities and the asset classes is 50 percent. Again, security selection is more important; the relative volatility between the assets is 10 percent, and between the asset classes, 8.66 percent.

Panel C shows that the asset class correlation has to be lower (33 percent versus 50 percent) for the relative volatilities to be equal and the relative decisions—asset allocation versus security selection—to be equally important. Finally, Panel D presents a case in which the asset allocation decision is more important than the security-selection decision. When the correlation of the securities is twice as high as the correlation of the asset classes, the asset allocation decision becomes the more important decision.

The Dispositive Answer. The dispositive answer to the question of which decision is more important, security selection or asset allocation, can be found through a simple experiment. My co-author and I resolved the issue by bootstrapping.

Bootstrapping is similar to Monte Carlo simulation, in which one randomly draws from a theoretical distribution. Bootstrapping randomly draws from an empirical distribution. For equities, we used the various MSCI country equity indexes for Australia, Germany, Japan, the United Kingdom, and the United States. For global bonds we used the J.P. Morgan Government Bond Index, and for global cash we used the J.P. Morgan Cash Index. We started by randomly selecting an individual stock out of the MSCI index for a given country; we calculated its return for the year 1988 and then put it back into the sample. Then, we shuffled the sample, chose again, calculated the return of a randomly selected stock, and replaced it. We continued until we had calculated the returns of 100 randomly selected stocks and had created a diversified portfolio. The portfolio did not necessarily have 100 different stocks, however, because we kept replacing the pick; so, the same stock could have been chosen more than once.

We calculated the average total return of the 100 stocks that were randomly selected. We then computed a portfolio return that assumed we had 60 percent allocated to these randomly selected stock portfolios, 30 percent allocated to a bond index, and 10 percent allocated to a cash index. For each year from 1989 through 2000, we repeated these six steps in portfolio composition 999 times. So, we had 1,000 portfolios that each had a 60/30/10 asset mix. The only characteristic that differentiated them was that they held different individual stocks.

The last step was to calculate the annualized cumulative returns of the 1,000 portfolios. The result was an empirical, although randomly generated, distribution of returns that was a product of security selection. In this manner, we were able to isolate the impact of security selection on the return distribution of the portfolios.

We then began a similar process whose objective was the generation of a random distribution of returns that was a product of asset allocation; in this case, the sample from which we randomly drew was composed of the equally weighted MSCI stock index, the J.P. Morgan Government Bond Index, and the J.P. Morgan Cash Index. The sample was weighted 60 percent toward the stock index, 30 percent toward the bond index, and 10 percent toward the cash index. As before, the total return of the randomly selected index was calculated and the selection was replaced. This process continued until 100 "assets" had been chosen and their respective returns selected. We calculated the average total return of these 100 assets. For each year from 1988 to 2000, we repeated each of these steps 1,000 times.

On average, therefore, the resulting portfolios had the same asset mix as the security-selection portfolios, but of course, because we chose randomly, we observed a lot of variation around that average. We ended up with 1,000 portfolios that contained the same individual securities within each asset class and had the same weights within each asset class but in which the asset allocation varied from 0 to 100 but was weighted toward 60/30/10.

What could be simpler? These tests should measure the importance of security selection by holding constant the asset mix and calculating the variation in wealth resulting from random security selection and the importance of asset allocation by holding constant the security weights and calculating the variation in wealth arising from random asset allocation. The answer, shown in **Figure 9**, is that a great deal more variation can be ascribed to portfolio returns based on the security-selection decision versus the asset allocation decision, even with very diversified stock portfolios. Figure 9 shows the 5th, 25th, 75th, and 95th percentiles of performance (the annualized difference from the average) of the 1,000 portfolios of Australian, German, Japanese, U.K., and U.S. securities from 1988 to 2000. A manager who is a top-quartile performer in any of these markets would be in the second band from the top of each bar—the larger bar for stock selection (SS) and the smaller bar for asset allocation (AA). Figure 9 shows clearly greater dispersion in returns from the stock-selection decision than from the asset allocation decision.

One could argue that this approach ignores risk. Suppose an investor does not care about how much wealthier a skilled investor can become by stock selection versus asset allocation. Rather, this investor cares about the peace of mind—the utility—that can be gained from investing, from making decisions based on security selection or asset allocation. To explore this scenario, we did a mean–variance approximation of a logwealth utility function.

The logwealth utility function is a standard utility function that is assumed in much of financial analysis. It can be approximated as follows:

$$U = \ln(1 + \mu) - \frac{1/2\sigma^2}{(1 + \mu)^2}, \quad (7)$$

where

U = utility
$\ln$ = natural logarithm
μ = annualized return
σ = annualized standard deviation

The utility function accounts for risk. **Figure 10** shows that even on a risk-adjusted basis, the stock-selection decision is much more important than the asset allocation decision.

The relative importance of the two decisions can actually be priced by assigning a specific value to the importance of stock selection and a specific value to the importance of asset allocation. The method uses

Figure 9. Return Potential from Security-Selection versus Asset Allocation: Simulation, 1988–2001 Data

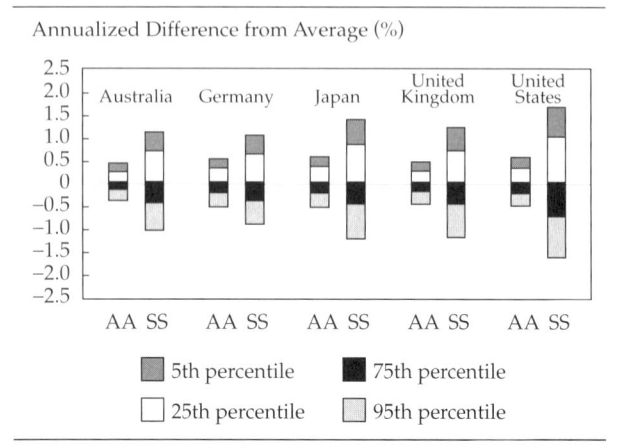

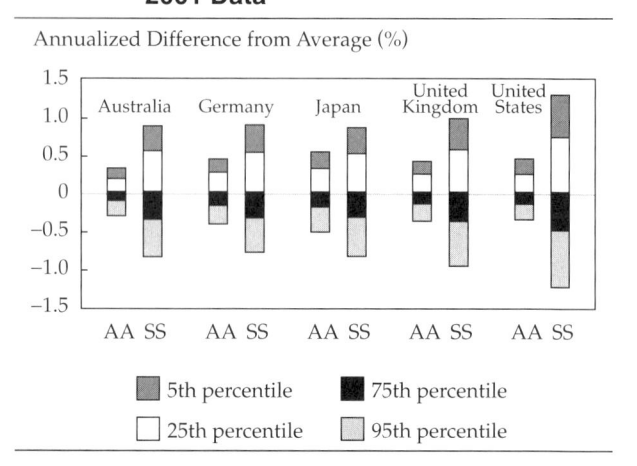

Figure 10. Utility from Security-Selection versus Asset Allocation: Simulation, 1988–2001 Data

an exchange option. The approach is to calculate an option to exchange median performance in security selection for top-quartile performance in security selection and to exchange median asset allocation performance for top-quartile asset allocation performance. This approach is then extended to the exchange of the bottom-quartile performance in security selection with the median performance in security selection and the bottom-quartile versus the top-quartile performance in security selection, and the same for asset allocation. This method gives the arbitrage-free price of exchanging one level of performance for another level of performance in security selection and in asset allocation.

For this test, we used the following equation:

$$EO = N(d_1) - N(d_2), \quad (8)$$

where

EO = value of the exchange option
$N(\bullet)$ = cumulative normal probability
$d_1 = \dfrac{\ln\left(\dfrac{V_P}{V_M}\right) + 1/2\sigma\varepsilon^2 t}{\sigma\varepsilon\sqrt{t}}$, in which ln denotes natural logarithm, V_P denotes starting value of the chosen percentile (bottom or top) portfolio, V_M denotes starting value of the median portfolio, and $\sigma\varepsilon$ denotes relative volatility between V_P and V_M
$d_2 = d_1 - \sigma\varepsilon\sqrt{t}$
t = time remaining to expiration, as a fraction of a year

The results for the countries shown in Figure 10 are in **Table 8**. In each panel, the first row provides the value of an option to exchange median performance for top-quartile performance and the second row provides the value of an option to exchange bottom-quartile performance for median performance. Panel A is for asset allocation, and Panel B is for security selection. For example, in the United States, the value of an option to exchange median for top-quartile performance in asset allocation is 63 percent, or 63 cents. The value of an option to exchange median for top-quartile performance in security selection in the United States is $2.70.

Panel C provides the relative value, the ratio of the option value of the security-selection decision to the option value of the asset allocation decision. This panel represents monetizing the relative importance of security selection versus asset allocation. It reveals that in the U.S. markets, for example, security-selection skill is 4.29 times as important as asset allocation skill. Moreover, an investor should be willing to pay almost 2.5 times as much to avoid bad security-selection results as he or she would be willing to pay to avoid bad asset allocation results.

Objections to the Dispositive Answer. Various objections could be raised to a number of aspects of the method I have just described. Following are these objections and my responses to these objections.

- *Security selection is occurring only within the stock component.* We did not have data for cash and bonds, so we did not include the individual securities in these indexes. Yet, if we had used such data and could have caused variation in performance by also randomly selecting bonds and cash instruments, our results would only be stronger. The additional data would amplify the dominant influence of security selection.

- *Attrition occurs in the early years in the MSCI indexes as stocks drop out, thus biasing the results.* This problem actually worked against us because a larger universe of individual securities would increase the importance of security selection in relation to asset allocation. A larger

Table 8. Relative Value of Asset Allocation and Security Selection

Percentile	Australia	Germany	Japan	United Kingdom	United States
A. Asset allocation					
Top quartile (%)	0.79	0.78	0.76	0.61	0.63
Bottom quartile (%)	0.43	0.64	0.45	0.50	0.81
B. Security selection					
Top quartile (%)	1.91	0.93	1.53	2.33	2.70
Bottom quartile (%)	1.14	1.35	1.66	1.63	2.01
C. Relative value					
Top quartile (×)	2.42	1.19	2.01	3.82	4.29
Bottom quartile (×)	2.65	2.11	3.69	3.26	2.48

universe would diminish the opportunity to affect wealth through asset allocation because the volatility of asset classes declines as securities are added.
- *Only the stocks that survived from 1988 to 2001 were included, so a potential problem of survivorship bias exists.* Our results may or may not be affected by the bias. To the extent that the performance of the deleted stocks was better than the surviving stocks, the simulation understates the potential importance of security selection.
- *In the asset allocation, equal weighting was assumed.* It is true that we used equally weighted indexes (because we did not have the capitalization weighting), so in the asset allocation, we were assuming equal weighting. This issue should not be important because cap-weighted indexes are less volatile, which means that using cap-weighted indexes reduces the relative volatility among the asset classes, but it also reduces the relative volatility among portfolios that differ by security composition. So, whether security selection or asset allocation would dominate if cap-weighted indexes were used is not clear. I do not think the substitution of cap-weighted indexes would significantly change the results.
- *The simulated stock portfolios represent unduly risky portfolios that few investors would be willing to own.* This charge is simply false. They are randomly selected security portfolios. They are well diversified; for example, the average tracking error of the top- and bottom-quartile portfolios that varied by security weights relative to the median portfolios is only 4.3 percent. It ranges from a low of 2.3 percent for Germany to 6.78 percent for the United States. Such portfolios are not unduly risky. Moreover, we found the same pattern when we used the dispersion of utility, which takes risk into account, as we did when we used wealth. If portfolios that vary by security exposure are so risky, we would expect to see significant compression in the distribution when we carried out the comparison in utility units as opposed to wealth units.
- *The portfolios that varied by security composition contrast the best stocks against the worst stocks and, therefore, represent unrealistic extremes.* Again, this charge is false. We did not first rank the securities from best to worst and then identify top and bottom portfolios; we contrasted the top percentiles with the bottom percentiles based on randomness. This is the distribution that occurs naturally in the capital markets. So, if investors do not consciously restrict tracking error, the distributions that I showed from security selection reflect the distributions of the opportunity set that exist naturally.
- *Finally, perhaps adding value is simply easier to do through asset allocation than through security selection.* Maybe it is, maybe it is not. It does not matter. If asset allocation is easier than security selection, clearly investors should carry out asset allocation because avoiding bad security selection is more important than avoiding bad asset allocation.

Conclusion

Investors may be underestimating portfolio risk in two ways. First, a focus on end-of-period risk to the exclusion of within-horizon risk leads to underestimation. The probability of loss within the investment period is much higher than the probability of loss at the end of the period. In addition, within-horizon probability of loss does not go down with time; it goes up. In addition, investors underestimate VAR by assuming that portfolio returns remain lognormal when short selling is added to long portfolios. Finally, security selection is significantly more important than asset allocation because it has much greater potential to influence wealth or happiness.

Question and Answer Session

Mark P. Kritzman, CFA

Question: How do you reconcile Ronald Kahn's view of breadth with a preference for asset allocation over stock selection?[1]

Kritzman: What drives the relative importance of security selection is that with more securities, the opportunity for extreme outcomes increases and the relative risk between asset classes goes down. The asset classes become less volatile as individual securities are added, with everything else held constant.

This aspect clearly explains why security selection is more important. If we had 100 asset classes to choose from, I don't know how it would shake out, but in reality, we have to allocate among a few asset classes and among many, many securities. Individual stock portfolios that can hold up to 100 securities are a good representation of the realities of investing.

Question: If you need more skill when you are lacking breadth, why would you rotate between asset classes; why not hold asset class weights constant and do security selection within those asset classes?

Kritzman: It depends on the assumptions that are made about the correlations of the securities within the asset class and the correlations of the asset classes. One position is that investors do asset allocation because they think the inter-asset-class efficiency is much lower than the intra-asset-class efficiency. Many investors worry about the relative value of Security A versus Security B, but few worry about the relative value of stocks versus bonds versus cash. So, perhaps, the reason is efficiency. I'm not endorsing that position, but people do make that argument.

Question: The opportunity in security selection is one thing, but the skill required to realize that opportunity is another thing, so according to the skill and breadth proposition, don't you need more skill just to pick up those returns?

Kritzman: No. If you're assuming that one set of opportunities is efficient and the other is not efficient, you need less skill to succeed in the less-efficient set. Skill and efficiency are two sides of the same coin.

Question: In relation to Figure 10, do you have any view as to why the United States has the highest risk-adjusted performance in terms of stock selection?

Kritzman: What the U.S. markets have is the greatest dispersion in terms of stock performance. The answer is that there are more stocks to choose from within the United States than there are within the other countries. It relates directly to the issue of breadth.

Question: Do you think your results would be the same if you replaced asset classes with economic sectors or industry groups?

Kritzman: I think security selection would still be more important, but the difference would be less. Again, it probably has to do with the fact that those groups contain fewer securities.

Question: If you were trying to fix the level of tracking error that the plan sponsor would be exposed to, would the same solutions hold if you're trying to find the most efficient way of allocating 2 percent active risk?

Kritzman: If you say you're going to constrain the tracking error to be such and such an amount, then—by definition—you will compress the dispersion that comes from security selection.

On an almost philosophical plane, the way I like to think about it is that we look at all the investment opportunities out there in the capital markets in a certain way: We stratify investments by sectors, countries, industries, asset classes, and so on. Figure 10 says that if you look at the dispersion that occurs naturally from portfolios that are randomly and reasonably diversified (that is, no financial engineering is artificially compressing dispersion), you find, first, that the natural opportunity set from security selection is much greater than the natural opportunity set from asset allocation and second (if you take my results in conjunction with those of Brinson et al.) that, as an industry, we have artificially compressed the natural set of opportunities that the capital markets make available to us.

We've compressed the opportunity set because we face business risk. I'm not saying that we should necessarily do things differently. I think that managers and investors, in their heart of hearts, realize how hard it is to add value through security selection, so they limit the business risk associated with that activity. One way of thinking about it is that we have unskilled investors; another is that they are so skillful that the markets are efficient. But investors perceive that efficiency; therefore, their behavior, what Brinson et al. measured, shows security selection not to be important. Well, security selection is very important. It is so important that people don't do it because when they do, they risk going out of business.

---

[1] See Mr. Kahn's presentation in this proceedings.

Selected Publications

AIMR

Benchmarks and Attribution Analysis, 2001

Best Execution and Portfolio Performance, 2001

Core-Plus Bond Management, 2001

Developments in Quantitative Investment Models, 2001

Equity Research and Valuation Techniques, 2002

Ethical Issues for Today's Firm, 2000

Evolution in Equity Markets: Focus on Asia, 2001

Fixed-Income Management for the 21st Century, 2002

Global Bond Management II: The Search for Alpha, 2000

Hedge Fund Management, 2002

Investment Counseling for Private Clients II, 2000

Investment Counseling for Private Clients III, 2001

Investment Counseling for Private Clients IV, 2002

Investment Firms: Trends and Issues, 2001

Organizational Challenges for Investment Firms, 2002

Practical Issues in Equity Analysis, 2000

The Technology Industry: Impact of the Internet, 2000

Research Foundation

Common Determinants of Liquidity and Trading, 2001
by Tarun Chordia, Richard Roll, and Avanidhar Subrahmanyam

Country, Sector, and Company Factors in Global Equity Portfolios, 2001
by Peter J.B. Hopkins and C. Hayes Miller, CFA

Earnings: Measurement, Disclosure, and the Impact on Equity Valuation, 2000
by D. Eric Hirst and Patrick E. Hopkins

International Financial Contagion: Theory and Evidence in Evolution, 2002
by Roberto Rigobon

Real Options and Investment Valuation, 2002
by Don M. Chance, CFA, and Pamela P. Peterson, CFA

Risk Management, Derivatives, and Financial Analysis under SFAS No. 133, 2001
by Gary L. Gastineau, Donald J. Smith, and Rebecca Todd, CFA

The Role of Monetary Policy in Investment Management, 2000
by Gerald R. Jensen, Robert R. Johnson, CFA, and Jeffrey M. Mercer

Term-Structure Models Using Binomial Trees, 2001
by Gerald W. Buetow, Jr., CFA, and James Sochacki

The Welfare Effects of Soft Dollar Brokerage: Law and Economics, 2000
by Stephen M. Horan, CFA, and D. Bruce Johnsen